URBAN DEVELOPMENT WITH COMMUNITY INITIATIVES

RETROSPECT AND PROSPECT

URBAN DEVELOPMENT WITH COMMUNITY INITIATIVES

RETROSPECT AND PROSPECT

G.S. RAO

ATLANTIC PUBLISHERS AND DISTRIBUTORS

Published by
ATLANTIC PUBLISHERS AND DISTRIBUTORS
B-2, Vishal Enclave, Opp. Rajouri Garden, New Delhi-27
Phones : 5413460, 5429987
e-mail : info@atlanticbooks.com

Sales Office
4215/1, Ansari Road, Darya Ganj, New Delhi-02
Phones : 3273880, 3285873, 3280451
Fax : 91-11-3285873
web site : www.atlanticbooks.com

ISBN 81-7156-895-5

Typeset at
APD Computer Graphics, Delhi

Printed in India at
Mehra Offset Press, Delhi

FOREWORD

It is my honour and pleasant duty to write the Foreword to this book by Dr. G. Surya Rao. It is an honour because in my view, Dr. Surya Rao is one of the world's foremost practitioners of the art and science of community development (CD). Since he is such a modest man, this statement may come as a shock to him, but not to those who have known him and his work. This work has demonstrated that he has not only "talked the talk" but also has "walked the walk" of CD. Dr. Surya Rao has always been generous in sharing his insights and learnings but in this long awaited and very welcome volume, he is making his rich experience available to a wider audience. For all those who are truly interested in participatory development — whether fieldworker, planner or development theorist — there is much to be gleaned from a careful reading of this book. He takes you with him as he works out real life problems on the ground.

The principles underlying CD — felt needs, self-help and community participation — are once again in vogue in development circles. The problem is that while many development professionals have talked and written about these principles, few have had the experience of implementing them successfully on the ground. Dr. Surya Rao and his colleagues are among these few. For this reason, among others, this is a very timely volume. The author has spent most of his professional life doing community development. He began as a veterinarian in the early days of the rural CD programme in India; then he became a Block Development Officer. When the first government pilot projects on urban community development (UCD) were started, Dr. Surya Rao was put in charge of the Hyderabad Project. This is one of the only original pilot projects which is still operating. Not only has it survived, he and his original colleagues built a programme within the Municipal Corporation, with a limited staff and budget, which has become a national and international model of what the UCD approach can accomplish.

Despite their limited budget, or perhaps because of it, no need felt by the people was beyond their consideration. This was because it was the people, not the Project, who were ultimately responsible for meeting their own needs — with a little help, advice and facilitation by the Project. The book describes this process in detail in cases such as the auto rickshaw drivers' training. I remember telling them jokingly that they were forced to depend upon people's involvement; because the Project had such a limited budget, there was no other choice. They laughingly agreed, but there is a serious lesson here. If unlimited amounts of outside money had been available, the staff might not have perfected their extraordinary skills in identifying and harnessing existing community resources so effectively. After all, if a poor community needs a place for a nursery school, it seems much more efficient and humane simply to build it if you have the money in your budget; rather than asking them if they know of a spare room somewhere in the community which could be used. However, they might not feel a sense of ownership and they might feel that the Project should maintain it. Furthermore, the question is whether the Project would ever have enough money to build nurseries for every community that felt they needed one. This cash shortage, combined with their creativity and flexibility is the reason why no challenge daunted the Project staff and why their list of activities is so long and varied, rather than neat and tidy. It ranged from paying off moneylenders, to nursery schools, to self-help housing, to trips to Sri Lanka for slum dwellers. People's felt needs are not neat and tidy and limited to those that are listed in the customary development project plan.

In the late seventies, the Project aroused national and international attention with its Habitat programme, which involved thousands of poor families constructing their own houses with the help of individual bank loans. There was very little government investment besides additional staff. The story typifies the Project's approach even in this huge activity. When the state government issued "pattas" (deeds to the land) to 13,000 squatter families, the UCD Project accepted responsibility for facilitating the construction of houses by the families themselves. The Secretary of Urban Development was incredulous at first but Dr. Surya Rao respectfully convinced him that it was possible. When I learned that the Project had taken full responsibility, I was taken aback because I felt that they did not have the management and staff capacity for such an enormous task. Shri Rama Rao soon helped me understand the error of my ways. He said : "Dr. Sahib, don't worry. We will not be building any houses. Just as in Devanagar where there were 23 families, each built one house; here there are 13,000 families and each family will build one house." And so it happened. This book describes in detail how the Project helped it to happen.

This anecdote illustrates both the simplicity and complexity of the CD process. It also illustrates the faith — based upon experience — which the staff had in the process and in the people. This particular activity was literally a concrete demonstration of people's power when skillful workers organize them. The traditional approach to the construction of affordable housing for the poor would have taken years and involved countless planners, architects and engineers. And inevitably there would have been leakages of resources, the use of some substandard materials and probably dissatisfaction on the part of the resident users.

The Hyderabad CD approach avoided all three of these customary problems by putting responsibility directly into the hands of the ultimate residents. It was up to them to stay within their budget, to buy the best materials at the cheapest rates and to hire and oversee the skilled workers they needed. And if the walls cracked or the roof leaked, who else was there to blame ?

The beautiful simplicity and logic of this approach causes one to wonder why it is not more widely adopted. Part of the answer is, of course, that there is no profit in it for middlemen and contractors and various others. But more important is the fact that people with the experience, conviction and imagination of Dr. Surya Rao and his colleagues are in very short supply and often not situated high enough in bureaucratic prestige and power. Some Officials from other cities, having seen the success of

Habitat, tried to replicate it back home but they could not. It seems their eyes were on the houses, which were the end product of a long painstaking process; rather than on the process itself.

The process went like this. The field staff began by approaching people in slum communities and explaining the scheme. Then they asked whether they wanted to take part in it. If the people were interested, the staff gave them a set of ground rules with which every family had to agree in order for the community to take part. One of these rules astonished me because it seemed so bold and so arbitrary, at first. And yet it turned out to be at the heart of the community building process. The rule was that each family not only had to agree to dismantle its house and move temporarily to a vacant area, but also had to agree that each plot in the new settlement would be of equal size. This, despite the fact that there was great variance in the size of plots which people were occupying. In some communities it took many, many meetings, as the book recounts, before unanimity was reached on these issues. But it was reached and I am convinced that it strengthened immeasurably the sense of community and sharpened the skills of consensus building among the people. There are many fascinating stories of what happened during this process.

I have spoken in detail about the Hyderabad Project because it was here that the multifaceted possibilities of the UCD approach were so beautifully demonstrated. In the book, Dr. Surya Rao goes on from his account of Hyderabad to share his experience in the Urban Basic Services programme, with which he was associated as a UNICEF officer after his retirement from the Municipal Corporation. UNICEF, in collaboration with the Central and State Governments, began the UBS Programme in an effort to replicate the UCD approach with a special emphasis upon children and women. Eventually, the Central Government took responsibility for UBS, renamed it Urban Basic Services for the Poor (UBSP) and has expanded it to hundreds of towns and cities across the nation. In this volume, Dr. Surya Rao relates his experience with these programmes particularly in Andhra Pradesh and Orissa.

Thus this book is unique in yet another way. It spans successive stages in the expansion of a development programme: from a few pilot projects to a significant move toward universalization of the UCD approach. Throughout his account, the author puts a human face on the process by returning again and again to the stories of real people and the real problems with which the project is helping them deal.

I began by saying that it is my pleasant duty to write this Foreword. It is my duty because I shall always be indebted to Surya Rao and Rama Rao for deepening my understanding of the community development process. It is my pleasure because I feel that this book is a significant and unusual contribution to the literature on CD. Its basic message is : See what poor people can do with a little skilled and patient help.

WILLIAM J. COUSINS
FORMERLY SENIOR URBAN ADVISOR,
UNICEF

PREFACE

As rightly affirmed by Dr. William J. Cousins, Former Senior Advisor, UNICEF in his foreword, this book can be an unusual but significant contribution to the literature on Community Development. It explains, through the author's experiences, what people can do with the help some skilled and patient guidance. A community development worker is a catalyst to change the attitude and behaviour of the poor to become worthy future citizens. In the process the worker can also become more rightful in his/her own behaviour if he/she believes and acts on the old saying "practice before you preach."

The author believes, learning is a two-way process in which the worker can equally be benefitted from the other side, if only he/she is not proud and arrogant of his/her own wisdom.

Upliftment of the poor need not be a monopoly for the community development worker. Irrespective of profession or practice, one can contribute and work for the development of poor if only he/she has the basic instinct. This is vividly narrated in the author's experiences.

G. Surya Rao

ACKNOWLEDGEMENTS

This book is attempted with an ambition to give an insight into the functioning of the Urban Community Development Programme and to provide useful tips and clues to the field workers. The contents are totally backed by field experiences, some of which have ended in negative results too.

The author wishes to place on record the valuable co-operation, guidance and support given by the senior IAS Officers like Sri C.N. Shastry, Sri V.S. Ramakrishna, Sri K. Subrahmanyan, Sri Narendra Luther, Dr. V.K. Bawa, Sri Jayakar Johnson. He also thanks his own team of Project Officers, Deputy Project Officers, Community Organisers, Social Workers, Basti Sahayaks, and Community Volunteers, who have contributed for success of the programme, by toiling day in and day out, to its stage till 1980, when the author had opted for voluntary retirement. He thanks them all for extending their co-operation in this humble effort for Human Development.

Even after retirement from Government, the author by his position in UNICEF continued to involve himself in similar programmes like Urban Basic Services (UBS) and Urban Basic Services for the Poor (UBSP) both in Orissa and Andhra Pradesh for another decade. His achievements in this role are mainly due to the unstinted support and guidance given by Dr. William J. Cousins, Mr. Dev D. Chopra, Mr. Leo Fonseka, Dr. E.N. Katkar, Mr. Kazuo Inoue, Mr. T. Gopinath Menon and others. The author owes his grateful thanks to one and all of them.

Prof. D. Ravindra Prasad, Director and Sri D.G. Rama Rau, Training Consultant in Regional Centre for Urban and Environmental Studies, have contributed much for this volume to attain its present shape even though our original ambition to bring it out through joint effort was not fulfilled. The observations made by

Sri N. Ganesan, Retired Staff Correspondent, Hindu Daily through his visits to different towns, with the assignment given by UNICEF, added much content to this volume. The author owes them all very much for their valuable contribution.

Dr. D. Vasudeva Rao has been of help in formating the content as well as finding a Publisher. Sri Dev D. Chopra was also very handy in this regard. The author is grateful to both of them. So also to the M/s. Atlantic Publishers and Distributors, New Delhi who gave their full support to this venture.

This work until very recently remained an unfulfilled task because of inappropriate work atmosphere. This was to a great extent transformed otherwise with the help of Sri G. Ananda Rao, his Industrialist brother, to whom the author is greatly indebted. Smt. G. Anasuya patiently bore the brunt of her husband's work before the computer and his daughter, Smt. K. Swarupa Rambabu supported the author in his documentation work for which he feels very proud.

G. Surya Rao

CONTENTS

PART I

URBAN COMMUNITY DEVELOPMENT : A PEOPLE'S PROGRAMME IN HYDERABAD

PART II

GROWTH OF UCD OVER TIME

ABBREVIATIONS

APSEB	:	Andhra Pradesh State Electricity Board
APUD & HC	:	Andhra Pradesh Urban Development and Housing Corporation
ANM	:	Auxiliary Nurse Midwife
APSHC	:	A.P. State Housing Corporation
B.V.Sc.	:	Bachelor of Veterinary Science
B.S.	:	Basti Sahayak
B.D.O.	:	Block Development Officer
B.T. Road	:	Bitumin Top Road
C.D.	:	Community Development
C.O.	:	Community Organiser
C.C.F.	:	Christian Children's Fund
CASP	:	Community Aid and Sponsorship Programme
C.D.S.	:	Community Development Society
C.D.O.	:	Community Development Officer
C.S.W.	:	Council for Social Welfare
C.B.O.	:	Community Based Organisation
C.H.V.	:	Community Health Volunteer
C.D.M.A.	:	Commissioner & Director of Municipal Administration
DWCRA	:	Development of Women & Children in Rural Areas
DWCUA	:	Development of Women & Children in Urban Areas
DUDA	:	District Urban Development Agency
EIUS	:	Environmental Improvement in Urban Slums
E.O.	:	Extension Officer

HUDCO	:	Housing and Urban Development Corporation
HSIP	:	Hyderabad Slum Improvement Project
HRD	:	Human Resource Development
HMWSSB	:	Hyderabad Metropolitan Water Supply & Sewerage Board
ICDS	:	Integrated Child Development Scheme
IPP	:	India Population Project
IAS	:	Indian Administrative Service
J.J. Act	:	Juvenile Justice Act
L.C.S.	:	Low Cost Sanitation
M.Ex.	:	Masters in Extension
M & E	:	Monitoring and Evaluation
MCH	:	Municipal Corporation of Hyderabad
M.L.A.	:	Member of Legislative Assembly
N.E.S.	:	National Extension Service
N.G.O.	:	Non Governmental Organisation
N.S.S.	:	National Service Scheme
N.R.Y.	:	Nehru Rozgar Yojana
NLMC	:	National Literacy Mission
N.P.A.	:	National Plan of Action
NDC	:	Neighbourhood Development Committee
NEDCAP	:	Non Conventional Energy Development Corporation of A.P.
NHC	:	Neighbourhood Committee
NFE	:	Non Formal Education
NABARD	:	National Bank of Rural Development
ODA	:	Overseas Development Administration
PMIUPEP	:	Prime Minister's Integrated Urban Poverty Eradication Programme
PVP	:	Prajala Vaddaku Palana
P.O.	:	Project Officer
QQDA	:	Quli Qutubsha Development Authority

RCV	:	Resident Community Volunteer
SHASU	:	Scheme of Housing and Shelter Upgradation
SUME	:	Scheme of Urban Micro Enterprises
SUWE	:	Scheme of Urban Wage Employment
SWOT	:	Strengths, Weaknesses, Opportunities and Threats
SJSRY	:	Swarna Jayanti Shaheri Rozgar Yojana
SIP	:	Slum Improvement Programme
SNP	:	Special Nutrition Programme
SVP	:	Shramik Vidya Peeth
SDO	:	Slum Development Officer
S.W. Drain	:	Storm Water Drain
S.S. Flooring	:	Shabad Stone Flooring
SMTD	:	Small and Medium Town Development
SUDA	:	State Urban Development Agency
SETWIN	:	Self-Employment in Twin Cities
TLMC	:	Town Level Management Committee
TTF	:	Town Level Task Force
T.V.	:	Television
UCD	:	Urban Community Development
UBS	:	Urban Basic Services
UBSP	:	Urban Basic Services for the Poor
UPAP	:	Urban Poverty Alleviation Programme
UK	:	United Kingdom
UWEP	:	Urban Wage Employment Programme
USA	:	United States of America
UPACOR	:	Urban Poverty Alleviation Corps
UPEC	:	Urban Poverty Eradication Cell
UFW	:	Urban Family Welfare
UPA	:	Urban Poverty Alleviation
ULB	:	Urban Local Body
VGRS	:	Voluntary Garbage Removal Scheme

LIST OF PHOTOGRAPHS

PART I

URBAN COMMUNITY DEVELOPMENT : A PEOPLE'S PROGRAMME IN HYDERABAD

1

Genesis of Urban Community Development (UCD)

The first experiment in UCD was initiated in 1958 in Delhi with the help of Ford Foundation with a Community Development approach already under practice in rural India from October 2nd, 1952, coinciding with the 83rd birth anniversary of the Father of the Nation, Mahatma Gandhi. Much earlier to this, the pre-independent India experienced several movements carried out by great visionaries and voluntary organizations to alleviate the sufferings of the masses from the ills of poverty, ignorance and disease. All these programmes mobilized human resources on a large scale to improve their living conditions.

The Delhi UCD project of 1958 was followed by the first series of UCD projects started in Ahmedabad (1962), Baroda (1965) and Calcutta (1996).

The Third five-year plan (1965-70) drew pointed attention to the social and economic consequences of the rapid growth of urban population. The plan laid particular emphasis on the need and potentialities of UCD for bringing about social and economic changes in urban communities and create conditions for a better life for its citizens.

The major interventions by Government over the period for the betterment of slum conditions all over the country include :

Slum Clearance Programme in 1956

Urban Community Development (UCD) in 1967

Environmental Improvement of Slums (EIUS) in 1972

Urban Integrated Child Development Services (ICDS) in 1975

Integrated Development of Small and Medium Towns in 1979 (IDSMT)

Urban Basic Services Programme in 1985 (UBS)

Urban Basic Services for the Poor in 1990 (UBSP)

Prime Minister's Integrated Urban Poverty Eradication Programme (PMIUPEP) in 1995

Swarna Jayanti Sheheri Rojgaar Yojana from 1997 (SJSRY)

The Rural Urban Relationship Committee (RURC)

After careful observation of the earlier projects and experiments, a Rural-Urban Relationship Committee was set up by the Ministry of Health, Government of India to plan and initiate Urban Community development projects on a nation-wide scale specifying the role of local bodies while implementing them.

The committee observed that there was lack of awareness and interest among urban poor and suggested the need to motivate change and encourage people to exercise their own initiative in planning and carrying out improvement projects based on their felt needs. Technical and welfare resources would then be directed to these communities to support them in their effort.

UCD Pilot Projects

On the basis of the recommendations of the RUR committee, the Government of India initiated the urban community development programme on an experimental basis. Originally planned for forty cities, pilot projects were finally taken up in 14 cities. Some State Governments were not enthusiastic in supporting this experiment and consequently seven were closed down, and of the remaining seven projects, Hyderabad is one with a continuous history of success in implementation and expansion of the Urban Community Development programme.

Guiding Strategies

The project addressed itself to human development by adhering to certain basic principles. It advocates that the ever increasing gap between the demand and provision of civic services in the growing cities can only be bridged by creating and making the best use of abundant resources and energies that can be tapped from the people themselves. The project creates stronger communities in problematic urban areas with their own leaders, who could plan and carry out self-help projects. Community organizations have proved to be the backbone of Urban Community Development Project.

The staff was given enough freedom to develop activities according to the felt needs of the people and was given a mandate to cover activities not normally in the ambit of the Municipal Corporation of Hyderabad. Thus it became a people's programme in the Municipal Corporation of Hyderabad, bringing the communities closer to the Local Body.

The objectives of Urban Community Development as defined in the scheme are as follows :

(a) To create a sense of social coherence on a Neighbourhood basis through corporate civic action; and promoting a sense of national integration.

(b) Develop a sense of belonging to the Urban Community through increased participation of people in community affairs, and promoting a way of thinking that they should concentrate first on solving problems with their own initiative, organization, self-help and mutual aid.

(c) To bring about a change in attitude by creating civic consciousness and by motivating people to improve their conditions of life.

(d) Developing local initiative, identifying and training local leaders.

(e) Ensure fuller utilization of technical and welfare services by helping the community to locate what help can be had from the Municipality or other organizations and how to get it; and what assistance and guidance can be obtained from governmental organisations and higher levels and how to approach them.

The Philosophy of the Programme

Self-help has been the philosophy of the Urban Community Development Project since the beginning. The project proceeded on the assumption that any neighbourhood, no matter however poor, can do something to improve itself by its own efforts and that any approach for outside help should be resorted to, only after it has exhausted its own resources fully.

This was not always an easy message to get across to poor people who sometimes felt that the Government should freely meet their needs because they were poor. Further, the project's desire to be thought of as a "People's Project" may also have posed difficulties because it was, after all a Government project. Basically it was the intention of the project to encourage people to identify their own felt needs and be involved fully in meeting them. It was hoped that through a process of community education and community self-help action, people's lives could be enriched and improved.

✪

2

Selection of Project Areas and Expansion

(a) Criteria for selection of town/city

- Interest evinced by the urban local bodies.
- Availability of voluntary organizations willing to cooperate with the experiment.
- Willingness of local body to provide funds for field programmes of a participatory nature with a non-conventional approach.
- Size and composition of the town.

(b) Criteria for selection of project area in the town/city

- Compact unit co-terminus with the mohalla/ward etc.
- Identical characteristics and level of services so that people will have some commonality of interests.
- Existence of area specific plans by the municipality.
- Willingness of local leaders to cooperate.
- Should cover few slums/congested areas/low-income communities in the old city/slum rehabilitation colony.
- Availability of public buildings or community halls.
- Focus on poor women, and children.

(c) For expanding the programme to two additional projects in Hyderabad the following were the considerations while selecting the area

- Popular demand and cooperation from municipal councilors.

- Existence of more number of slums/poor urban pockets.
- Weaker section areas where house site pattas (title deeds) were granted to the dwellers.
- Slums in which municipal corporation has planned to implement environmental improvement programme.
- Spreading the programme to the new city and Secunderabad, north of Musi river, was also a consideration as one project is already there in the old city on the southern side.

Accordingly two projects were started in 1974 in Secunderabad and Musheerabad.

Finally when the programme was extended to the entire twin cities with UNICEF assistance in 1978, the project covered all the slums in the city with a population of over 5 lakhs. The project was a small wing in Municipal Corporation of Hyderabad (MCH) acting as a link and liaison between welfare and developmental departments, city level voluntary organisations and the people.

✪

3

Selection of Functionaries — Original Project

The pilot project envisaged that at the experimental stage, it would be necessary to have more competent, adequately qualified and trained organizers and high level directing staff. The first team consisted of a project officer (PO) and eight community organizers (COs) (four males and four females). The PO was a Selection Grade Block Development Officer and the COs were Social Education Organizers. They were all people with experience in Rural Community Development and were selected by the Government by open advertisement and invitation. It is a well balanced team with all positive attributes, which contributed to the success of the programme.

Expansion

The objective was to make the programme as inexpensive as possible and expansion programme does not mean proportionate expansion of staff. As such, when the programme was extended, the members of the original team headed the new projects as Deputy Project Officers. Later with the launching of the Habitat scheme and the Integrated slum improvement project covering all wards in Municipal Corporation of Hyderabad, a Director's post was created and the Project Officer of the pilot Project was made the Director and the Community Organizers as project officers and Deputy project officers.

The new projects were run with the assistance of voluntary social workers hand picked by the Deputy project officers on honorarium basis. Similarly at the community level, the balwadi teachers, the craft masters etc. were also voluntary workers. In the earlier period, they were engaged by the project with the consent of the local communities and later on, these voluntary workers were engaged by the local community organizations with the consent of the project. Earlier the project paid the honorarium directly to the community voluntary workers and in the later stages the honorarium was paid to them through the local community organizations. This was meant to give the feeling to the communities that they are the real implementers of the programme and the workers engaged are their own with freedom to dispense with their services depending upon the actual need and performance of individual workers. This sort of community management facilitates availability of ample services to local communities, which the governmental agency cannot think of. For *e.g.* one balwadi is required for every 1000 population to cater to children of 3-6 years age group. It is impossible for any bureaucracy both financially and administratively to create so many institutions. The honorarium was Rs. 50 per month which was enhanced to 75, 100, 150 and Rs. 200 over a period of time and these workers are preferred to be middle aged and locally available with sufficient leisure time and aptitude to serve the fellow citizens. In these days of acute unemployment, youngsters may be tempted to creep into these temporary assignments, which has to be staunchly discouraged, as it will spoil their future career.

When the Habitat scheme was taken up in 1976, 80 posts of new functionaries, designated as Basti Sahayaks (slum helpers) were created. Basti Sahayaks (BS) are multipurpose workers and each BS has to cover about 100 houses. He/She has to be a matriculate. As the honorarium was fixed at Rs. 200 per month, the project was asked to call for candidates through employment exchange as per the prevailing rules. Out of the candidates sponsored by the employment exchange, the best were selected. This nullified the original intention of making the slum families choose their own representative direct from the slum itself as Basti Sahayak.

Meanwhile service rules for the project staff *i.e.* Director, Project officers, Deputy project officers and community organizers were framed by the government, which made the Municipal commissioners and other subordinate staff of the Municipal

Corporation eligible to the project posts. Accordingly the vacancies arising from time to time and the new posts were filled from these cadres. The posts of the first three projects were made permanent and the Urban Community Development project has thus become a permanent department in the Municipal Corporation of Hyderabad.

As time passed, the Basti Sahayaks agitated for scales of pay and change of designation as slum development officers, and succeeded. This trend made the other voluntary workers, who are working as balwadi teachers and sewing teachers (about 250 of them) who continued for years as volunteers also organized into a Union for regular scales of pay. To be ideal, an organization like UCD can only be an apex body which stimulates, supports and guides the local communities to organize themselves into strong groups and manage their own affairs from A to Z. The Government must be willing to delegate all community level functions to these groups. Does it mean losing grip and delegating all powers? Even then it is a must to stimulate community action and minimize external interference.

Selection of Workers

Core Staff

An unwilling worker amongst the core staff is more a nuisance and a negative load to the UCD. Selection methods have to be suitably innovated to get the right person for the job and educational qualifications should not be the only criterion for selection.

The worker's attitude, willingness to work for the poor, and temperament have all to be assessed before recruiting him to the project. A rigorous evaluation is compulsory after one year, which should decide whether he could be continued. In this case, sympathy and pity will only augur the programme downfall. As in private enterprise, in many developed countries, the system of contract appointment with attractive remuneration may be tried. Maturity of thought and mind is essential in this case and age need not be a restriction while selecting the candidates, if they have shown sufficient experience in voluntary service sector earlier.

4

Communities and Community Worker

Communities

Some of the distinctive features which were apparent in the past are undergoing a distinct change now. The old leadership patterns are not often perceptible and individual families tend to be self-centred. The social bondages between families in some communities remain weak. It will be a hard task for the community worker to identify the potential leaders to work for community cohesiveness by creating common interest for the community as a whole. In many communities there may be several selfish leaders who always adopt a divide and rule policy or create different types of unrest and rivalry, which ruptures the entire community structure. The role of the community worker would be to identify and deal with such of them in an amicable way.

Just like oasis in the desert, we still have some exemplary communities, where the leaders as well as followers have mutual regard and respect thus making them quite identical in confirmation to our old definitions. In the weaker section communities, there are often more needs to be accomplished and so they tend to be more homogeneous with a strong leadership pattern. But at times, it may be more dictatorial and it does not tend to promote or nurture democratic values. This situation can conveniently be transformed by the community worker in the right direction if he can help the members to make a SWOT (strengths, weaknesses, opportunities and threats) analysis and work for corrective action. In urban area situation the communities are very complex and heterogeneous and the common interests, group thinking and behaviour are no longer distinctive. The individual families within the community are alien to each other in these days and there will be the absolute need to create some binding activity by an extraneous work force.

In periurban areas with predominantly agricultural occupation, urban characters are gradually becoming more conspicuous and the traditional and religious patterns, which were in vogue earlier, become scarce commodities now.

Community Work

Community work has to be guided by the following basic principles which should be well conceived and rightly taken care of by the worker at every juncture.

A. **Community participation :** This indicates the degree of success in working with communities and without this the vital meaning of and the basic objective behind community work is lost.

B. **Convergence :** The community worker cannot work in isolation. His success depends more on the cooperation and support that he gets from other agencies to cater to community needs. The feeling of 'I' should not prevail in the community worker's mind.

C. **Cost effectiveness :** The community workers should always watch out and judge whether the programme is low budgeted evoking maximum people's response, whether it is going to be well utilized and whether maintenance and upkeep of the end product is assured. Here we have enough examples like community latrines, community halls etc. on which huge amounts have been spent; but left useless as nobody's concern. I still recollect one corporation community hall in a slum where cows were happily taking rest in the verandah and the other one in contrast in the same colony — humble, simple and low cost; but with an element of pride blooming in the faces of the people, who worked for it and feel it is theirs. The criterion is not the money but the willing effort of the community behind it.

D. **Continuity :** The worker must motivate and keep the community in good spirit at all times so that they always look for new accomplishments in addition to sustaining and upkeeping the old ones. For this a strong and well knit organisation at community level is very important. Since early 80's, UNICEF, in which I was a humble contributing force, was advocating Neighbourhood Committee approach and the results we had with over 2000 such committees in Orissa and Andhra Pradesh in the recent past was quite rewarding. But again it is not the number, that is taken into account by the bureaucracy usually, that is important or useful. It is the quality and the process through which they are formed and the continuous backup training to enhance their capacity is very important. I visited few states sometime ago, where I found not to my surprise, that these committees are only on paper and not on ground due to various reasons. A true Community worker should sincerely try to avoid such pitfalls and he must be given sufficient time to work for their systematic formation and composition.

E. **Coverage :** The aim of community worker should be to work for poor, women and children, who are the neglected lot. We have the category of wise and shrewd innovators at one extreme, who always try to grab every opportunity to live better and those of laggards at the other extreme, who are least motivated and survive in a deplorable way on Karma theory.

The Community worker can get easy and quick results by working with the former groups; but it will be something like breaking his head against a rock to work with the latter group. He must always try to keep a balance and use the motivated group as example to uplift the living conditions of the deprived. This requires tact, patience and perseverance for the worker, even though the results are far-reaching. We had a slum community with ST population in the midst of one of the posh localities about two decades ago when I was the Director of UCD in Hyderabad. The elite of the locality are themselves top bureaucrats or very close to them and they somehow wanted to avoid this nuisance of drunkenness, quarrels etc., in their vicinity. An alternate site was acquired nearby and UCD was asked to motivate and convince this community to accept this new site for their houses. This was smelt by the slum community and they were stubborn in spite of sincere efforts by our community workers and they even wielded their cudgels and threatened them not to come on this mission once again. We felt we have to identify and mix ourselves well with the community to minimize the social distance from them. We are sure their life pattern will change if they accept our new proposal. So on one fine morning, we collectively decided to camp for a night on a festival day in the slum joining them in some religious programme. So we sent word to the community few hours in advance, took our dinner boxes and had an interesting social gathering with the slum people. We did it finally, slept and got up in the morning, used some neem twigs for our mouth wash and enjoyed morning hospitality with Chai. Then went back with no discussion whatsoever. That was the beginning of a good housing programme with self-help bank loan assistance.

Community Work — A Slow Process?

Community work might look like a slow process in the initial stages. But if the approach is right and if the community is well organised and guided, things can move fast. Against the rigid municipal rules, UCD was able to promote 3 housing colonies in slums in spite of the unfavourable bank lending policies and rigid municipal building rules. This demonstrated as to how the living conditions of the poor can be improved with their own effort if sufficient stimulus and encouragement is given by external agencies, be it NGO or government. This triggered the government to give 13,000 house sites for poor in slums followed by the massive self-help housing with bank loan assistance and later by HUDCO. One top level engineer said 'You need a massive engineering and city planning cell to undertake this work estimated to cost over Rs. 5 Crores.' We desisted the move and managed with few supervisors and town planning staff and showed a big difference between a governmental work and a community work.

To motivate the first few slums, the community workers had to put in a lot of effort; but as it moves, demonstration in a developing site and facilitating free and frank dialogue amongst the peer groups has speeded the work.

UCD was a small section in Municipal corporation with hardly 8 community organizers and a project officer. But its performance in housing was commendable and much more than what a mighty government department could have done.

The community worker must ensure and go by 3 important thumb rules — speed and spontaneity, economy and self-help. He must strike the iron when it is hot and act with speed. Otherwise he cannot catch up with the enthusiasm of the communities, which may be instantaneous and short-lived. For this he must have simultaneous support from his bosses also. This requires him to be in the direct vision of his higher-ups, whether they need him or not and alert them on various ongoing programmes. They always tend to give least preference to this type of low budgeted programme and they might also have their own impressions out of previous exposures. These should not discourage the community worker and should seriously work for their cooperation and support at every level. This reminds me of my being often branded as post-ratification officer as I used to be forced to make promises in the field first and then seek post approval on files. You must create such confidence in your bosses.

Need for Community Work

Communities exist

They have potential for improvement

Life has increasingly become competitive and commercial for which a solution has to be found out.

They know their problems and needs better

Increasing population and marginalisation

Inadequacy of basic services

Exploitation of certain sections by power groups

Breakdown of family systems leading to generation gap

Exposure to consumerism and commercialisation

Environmental imbalances

Social inequalities

Communities in displacement and transition

Lack of awareness, concern and illiteracy.

Community Work and Turnover of Bosses

In government, the turnover of bosses is often high due to transfers and promotions. Everytime the boss is changed, the community worker has to be a motivator. For this the past impression of him, his credibility and the way the second rank officers in the organisation treat and evaluate him are very important. Long ago in the early 70's, there was a very senior officer at state level, who frankly told that his impressions on community work are not positive; but he heard much about Hyderabad programme. So he said, he would like to spend about 3 hours on one morning in the field with us to make his own assessment. As we moved and had discussions with the communities, he got so engrossed and interested that he actually spent 9 hours with them. From then on he became a staunch advocate for community development work and you will be surprised a stage had come when he and another senior officer had a tug of war on who should own this programme and implement it under his guidance and direction.

The Political Forces

The political forces also tend to keep the communities in utter confusion thereby sabotaging the community feeling. Government is considered to be the provider for all their basic needs, which may or may not materialize. But still the communities deliberately and demandingly wait for them thereby the spirit of self-help and community effort is diminished. Various governments, of late are realising that community participation, group work and community management are vital for sustaining any programme and make it lively. It is for the bureaucracy and different political groups to get attuned to that philosophy and the community worker has to play his humble role to promote this at grass-root level.

The community worker must try to start from where the people are in terms of their attitudes, needs and aspirations. He should not feel it is an assignment or a ritual; but he must be emotionally involved in it and derive real joy through working with people. He must be one with them in their joys and sorrows. I am reminded of a community worker in Orissa, who really practiced what is preached and commanded much love and affection. When he fell ill and got admitted in a hospital, people took turns to care and attend on him. Such should be the reciprocity.

Human development has to be in terms of enhancing individual and group capacity and aiming at democratic leadership. Government is not generally attuned to this objective as it may undermine its own value and importance, which it does not much relish. When planning, all this is generally laid down; but not necessarily carried out.

Agencies like Non-governmental organisations (NGOs) must be encouraged in a big way and Government intention should be to minimise its role and interference at community level adapting delegatory procedures to the maximum possible extent.

The Urban Community Development programme advocated community self-survey using simple formats contrary to routine official survey. This enables the communities to vividly understand where they are and how they should proceed further.

Delegation of Power

Community development is a process in which the local communities are motivated or a conscious decision is initiated by the authorities to delegate or transfer responsibilities to people and thus initiate a welcome beginning of enabling people to manage their affairs in their own humble way. Is the bureaucracy or the existing political structure ready to relinquish minimum powers to community based organisations or do they feel they do not wish to lose their importance and always want people to crave for mercy and help, however simple and silly it might be? Will it be offered or has it to be demanded? The community worker has a role to play in both situations.

Profile of a Community Worker

1. The worker helps in building rapport, acceptance, respect and understanding between the members and between the worker and the members.
2. He plays supporting and stimulating role.
3. The worker provides guidance and floats new ideas.
4. The worker has the problem-solving role.
5. The worker has to undertake most of the responsibility for programme.
6. The worker's role also includes observation and interpretation of the activities in the group.
7. Limiting and controlling over-aggressive members.
8. He involves in group activities all members including less and non-participatory members.
9. He resolves conflicts in a manner which would be acceptable to all concerned.

Attributes of a Community Worker

(i) As an Educator consolidates their thinking.

(ii) As an Animator kindles and sustains the interest of the members in issues important to the community.

(iii) As a Catalyst helps the members to identify community needs and line up resources to meet these needs.

(iv) As a Therapist helps those in need of help.

(v) As an Advocate pleads the cause of individuals and groups before welfare or development agencies. He also interacts with policy-makers and programme-planners in order to enhance the reach and effectiveness of development policies and programmes.

(vi) As an Activist, the worker would mobilize individuals and groups for collective action.

Activity Workers at Community Level

What is offered to them is just an honorarium, which is not adequate to a person, who thinks it is his/her job. On humanitarian grounds, if a matriculate unemployed young girl is taken for this work, it amounts to spoiling her career, as she cannot put her mind for a permanent avocation to support her future. A housewife with one or two children, with middle school education and maturity in age is the right choice, as she takes it as a leisure time activity to fetch some extra income to her family. The local organisation is the agency to engage all these workers and they shall be the paymasters too. If the municipal chief is eager to expand his empire by bringing them to his rolls, they are bound to claim regular employment status in the municipality, which will lead to chaos. These workers are not accountable to the NHC also thereby promoting inefficiency.

✪

5

Training and Financial Co-operation

For the first time, the original team of 9 functionaries (one P.O. and 8 COs) received two months' training at the Faculty of Social Work at M.S. University, Baroda before starting the project, after they were provisionally selected. Later on they attended short-term refresher training in the Tata Institute of Social Work, Bombay. But for this, there was no formal training to any member of the staff later. The new staff got training on the job by working with the old staff who is experienced. However there were few attempts made for training the functionaries as follows :

1. As and when the International Youth Centre (Viswa Yuvak Kendra), New Delhi announced programmes, the Municipal Corporation deputed staff and youth leaders. This training proved to be useful for inspiring the staff and youth leaders to broaden their horizons of imagination and thinking.
2. When the Habitat scheme was launched, the project team has designed and conducted a training programme for the Basti Sahayaks for about a week, at a place outside the city (Gram Sevaks Training Centre, Rajendranagar) making it a residential course. This training was useful to impress upon the refreshers about their role in the programme.
3. After UNICEF intervention, an Institution (Princess Esin Educational Society) was identified, which was giving one week training to the balwadi teachers every year during summer vacations. Earlier, voluntary workers like balwadi teachers and sewing teachers were trained

through monthly centre classes, where teachers in rotation give model lessons followed by constructive criticism from colleagues and staff took model classes.

4. Two reorientation workshops on UCD plan of action with UNICEF assistance were conducted for all the staff.
5. Community leaders training programmes were conducted twice with the assistance of voluntary organizations led by Mr. Allen Bachelor.
6. Members of Mahila mandals (women's groups) were given series of training in Food and Nutrition with the cooperation of the demonstration units of the Department of Food and Nutrition, Government of India.
7. After the SIPS were taken up by the UCD, regular training programmes were started through the Regional Centre for Urban and Environmental Studies; Osmania University, Hyderabad and U.K. based development-planning unit with ODA assistance.

Financial Cooperation (from State, Municipal Corporation and other Agencies)

Originally when the project was started in 1967 the annual budget was Rs. 65,000 for a population of 50,000 including a grant of Rs. 15,000 as matching assistance for local programmes. The Government of India, State Government and MCH shared the expenditure in the ratio 2 : 1 : 1. After three years (in 1970) the project was transferred to the State Government which continued to meet 75% of the cost. The programme was originally limited to 22nd ward of the city. With additional demands from other wards, the project area was first extended to about 20000 urban poor in the nearby 17th ward with an additional allotment of Rs. 15,000 for matching assistance for local programmes which was entirely met by the Municipal Corporation with no additional staff.

The Municipal Corporation realized the usefulness of this programme and requested the Government to expand it to the entire twin cities expressing its readiness to meet 50 per cent of the cost instead of 25 per cent which was committed in the first project. The Government sanctioned two more projects in 1974 at a cost of Rs. 1.50 lakhs per annum to be shared equally between the State Government and MCH. In the next stage when the scope of the UCD programme was enlarged with the introduction of HABITAT housing programme in 1976, banks came forward in a big way to advance loans for housing purpose while the Government increased its allocation for environmental upgradation in all the housing colonies taken up by the UCD project. The programme was further expanded to 9 projects in 1978 to cover the entire urban poor in twin cities with additional assistance from UNICEF.

Thus there has been a steady and continuous growth of the programme in all directions and the municipal corporation and the State Government as well as other agencies like banks and voluntary organizations came forward with increasing participation and funding. Subsequently, the housing programme was further enlarged from 1981 drawing loan assistance from HUDCO with Government guarantee.

Later, in 1983-84, UCD, MCH attracted massive grants running into crores of rupees from the ODA, UK Government for implementing its successive slum improvement projects.

6

Activities with a Difference

The Humble Beginnings and the Problems Faced

The implementation process is very important in this project. The people are the main actors here. They undertake to improve the quality of life in the community through their own initiative and action. Community organizers (COs) are only educators, motivators, helpers, enables facilitators and change agents to accelerate the process of change. The COs work with people, neither for nor instead of people.

It is a development process in which the people's capabilities are built by harnessing their own resources, leadership and community organization. They identify and articulate their felt needs and participate in designing the activities and implementing them with their own initiative and with outside help wherever necessary.

Conceptually, human development, through participation, is the ultimate aim. It is also the basis on which the project seeks to bring about long-term physical and economic improvement. The undercurrent of all the project activities is the involvement of people. None of the activities is a mono-focussed one.

For example, setting up basti (slum neighbourhood) development committees and Mahila Mandals (Women's organizations) are ways of working with communities through their own community members — they are the means for promoting self-help.

Study tours, exhibitions, film shows are not only ways of expanding the horizons of the participants, but are also means of drawing the community together — of fostering a 'WE' feeling.

Improving physical amenities is not only for improving people's living conditions, it is a way of calling community participation and create the sense — her programme is 'OURS'.

Housing is not just a family affair; the whole locality has to re-adjust, so as to plan houses for everyone in that locality; lay out is looked into by every one in the colony — it becomes a group effort. The guiding principles under the habitat housing became :

> "SELF-HELP IS OUR MOTTO
> *ECONOMY IS OUR WATCHWORD*
> QUICKNESS IS OUR THUMB RULE OF ACTION"

Underlying all the activities — ideally, if not always actually, is the idea of 'community' development — through guided and aided self-help and mutual cooperation.

Awareness creation was the primary task for the project staff in the initial stages; but except the skeletal staff, there was nothing of its own. It had to explore various departments and agencies, which had the manpower and necessary audio-visual equipment but no organization at the field level. The Urban Community Development (UCD) identified potential leaders in different communities, who are ready to render all support at the community level and make the programmes simmering with people's enthusiasm.

Using convergence effort with no cost from project, film shows, dance and drama programmes, seminars and symposia were organized on an intensive scale. These were not just routine and recreational but based on the expressed needs and tastes of different groups, assessed in advance through group discussions and individual contacts. Free and frank discussions immediately after these presentations developed direct contacts with resource persons concerned, which was a matter of great satisfaction for the beneficiary communities. The officers from various departments like Industries, Cooperation, Agriculture, Animal Husbandry, Education, Health, through these informal interactions, also developed a sense of special affinity which went a long way in cherishing their long range aspirations.

The project never went with a welfare attitude, volunteering to do everything to the people. But it intensified the visits and contacts to promote identity and friendship with different groups first which ultimately come out with "we need this; but we are unable to unite and work together" or "we do not know how to go about". Then came the facilitating role of Community Organizer who WORKS WITH THEM AND NOT FOR THEM for fulfilling their needs.

The emphasis all along has been that the communities are in the forefront and that process is more important than the product, which means, it should not be merely a number game. Keeping these broad guidelines in mind, several activities have been initiated in partnership with the communities and some of them are broadly narrated below.

In a Study Tour

Here the community and the leaders assume a lead role. An Organizing Committee was first formed consisting of members from different participating communities. They decide the places, number of days and the detailed itinerary. They meet the travel agency along with the community organizer, show the itinerary and take advice for a more economical proposition. The contract amount and dates are decided to suit the convenience of participants. The fare for each member is worked out to make the total collection nearly one and half times to that of the contract amount to cover accommodation and miscellaneous expenses on the way. Packed food was brought by the participants themselves to cut down the expenses. Letters are written in advance by the project to the agencies at other places indicating the visit and requesting for accommodation at low cost or no cost. Excellent camaraderie was built up through this tour. One and all equally shared joys and difficulties, again giving preference to women and children. To give an example on one tour the contract bus went into repairs and the whole team had to spend a night there on the way, where there was no habitation nearby. The group decided women and children should sleep inside the bus and the rest outside.

After the hectic trip, followed by a couple of days rest, a review meeting was called for in which the receipts and expenditure,

FANCY DRESS IN CHILDREN'S FESTIVAL

the study tour report were discussed. In recognition of selfless service by few participants token gifts were presented by the group. A letter of thanks was sent to different host agencies and one can imagine the participatory and learning experiences created through such tours. With faulty guidance, it can lead to a disastrous situation also. One quarter of travel cost from the project was enough to act as an incentive support to this activity, which provided much of inter and intra community cohesiveness.

Youth Festivals and Melas

These Festivals and Melas are to bring to light the inherent talents from within different groups, *viz.*, housewives, educated girls, pre-primary school children, youth, etc. They may be in terms of proficiency in education, teaching ability, home and environment management, games and sports, health habits, demonstrations, proficiency in skills, cultural talents, awards to best volunteers, etc. These Melas aim to remove all inhibitions and make them as one. From Local Welfare Association level all the way upto total city, competitions were held at various levels to give the benefit of participation to everyone. After thorough discussions on budget, city and mohalla level roles and expectations, clear cut instructions are developed from top to bottom indicating the budget, role of local organizations, city level and mohalla level committees which are formed specially for the purpose.

If all this was to be done by committees including money, management and prizes procurement, the role of project staff, was invisible and silent with remote controls. These committees meet only in the evenings to avoid dislocation of normal work to its members. The grandeur of this mela depended upon the degree of participation of communities and its groups and the support that it commands from outside agencies in which case, the project budget was very negligible. That was the beauty of this programme.

Creches in Slums

In one rehabilitated slum the project was inquisitive to know how children below 3 years are taken care of during daytime. For this a quick survey was thought of. Four volunteers were requested to go in different directions from a central point, contact each house and look for kids who are under care of elderly girls or old women. Each volunteer has covered over 20 families and they all identified 18 children 12 of whom were left under the care of girls and 6 under old women. The practice was that the mother keeps the food or milk in a small vessel and goes out to work. By next morning the Community Organiser was asked to buy and bring few toys, washing and toilet kits a few stainless steel tiffin boxes and milk bottles all costing around Rs. 150. The mothers of these 18 children and the caretakers were assembled at the community hall. They realised the following :

(a) the future of the elderly girls is spoiled because they are made to take care of the kids.

(b) The child is not looked after in an ideal way, because the girls know very little about sanitation, baby care etc.

(c) The elderly women can look after six children instead of one if some extra incentive is given.

(d) There is no need to have an ayah as the old women can do everything with some orientation.

(e) These infants need food, sleeping kits and food items and also some toys to play with. A bucket to store water, soap and a few towels, comb, etc. may also be made available to take care of the kids.

(f) If all these things are taken care of, the mother has no hesitation in paying about Rs. 10 every month to support the old women who take care of her kids thereby relieving the girl to attend her school.

When these mothers were sitting around with their children, some play material was pushed to the centre, which spurred all the kids to rush to them and engage themselves in play. Thus the idea of organising a creche with some extra support from project by way of play material, some supplemental nutrition etc. on a contribution basis took birth. In these creches, expensive cradles are not required. People know how to improvise them with baskets, jute bags and straw. All this is possible with little expenditure as against the ones organised by government with over Rs. 50,000 budget per annum.

Pre-schools etc.

For pre-schools, local skills centers and such other community based institutions, similar strategies to identify the beneficiaries and organise them with community involvement were also tried. Here the beneficiaries who are in need have to be identified, a local woman was selected for the job, decide on how much is the contribution from the beneficiary and how much assistance is required from project and where is the place to organise the activity. The only thing is that the caretakers have to be given some training in advance.

Community Latrines

Almost all-local bodies have spent millions to construct community latrines and they have excellent achievements in terms of numbers. When the question of proper maintenance and management comes, it became a matter of utter failure. No matter how much money was spent every month they remained as eye sores and centers of grave insanitation with lot of complaints from public. The reason is the users are least concerned with the maintenance and the municipality has to do everythings. UCD has a solution. Instead of municipality spending Rs. 1,000 on each latrine, it can as well sanction Rs. 400 to the local organisation entrusting that maintenance responsibility to it. This is tried with success in some cases. The organisation engaged a local person to clean the latrine and also insist the users to flush it immediately after use. These can be the instances where local body may fail but not the local organisation which can nicely get the latrine white washed and inscribe a slogan "This latrine is ours — let us all keep it clean". The latrine can no longer be an eye sore to the vicinity.

Supplementary Feeding Centres

In the Gandhi Centenary year, Government of India sanctioned about 200 supplementary nutrition centres to the Municipal Corporation but barely giving a fortnight's time for their launching. The Special Officer immediately called for a meeting of all the Section heads and asked how many centres can be organised by each section. The total put together could hardly come upto 30 centres and UCD agreed to organise the remaining centres within the stipulated time and the strength behind it is the vast number of voluntary organisations. It immediately called for a meeting of the voluntary organisation representatives to explain the task of identifying the beneficiaries, fixing up of organisers, helpers and accommodation and run the activities under their supervision. The municipal corporation has many sections with more than 15,000 employees out of which UCD is one with just eight staff members. This achievement by our small cell made the Special Officer appreciate the services at the Republic Day meeting and complimented it as the biggest little project in Municipal Corporation of Hyderabad.

Simple Marriages

In slums marriages are fixed by elders, and soon after that liquor is enjoyed by every one liberally. The same practice will continue during and after marriage. To do all this the elders borrow heavy amount at exorbitant interest (may be even Rs. 10 per 100 per month) and soon after the marriage, this loan burden is transferred to the newly wed couple, who has to struggle all through their life with lot of mental worry.

In a meeting of youth, this social evil was discussed and it was felt UCD should take a lead in celebrating the marriages in a simple way. Lime juice is prepared in a big vessel, a big leader (political or otherwise) is invited to bless the couple after the ritual is completed, few photos taken and the couple is given some utilities as gifts by some non-governmental organisations or charismatic persons. Youth from other communities are invited with a view that it will be replicated by them. These simple marriages have caught the imagination of every one.

Inter-caste and Inter-religious Marriages

These type of marriages were also supported by UCD through A.P. Kula Nirmulana Sangam for which one of our colleagues, Sri D.G. Rama Rao was the General Secretary. But the couples are always advised in advance not to think about marriage, until they are settled well in life with a befitting occupation. The Social Welfare Department in Government of Andhra Pradesh took this lead and started giving household articles as gifts to the couples from their funds as an incentive for inter-caste marriages to promote national integration.

Removal of Indebtedness amongst Municipal Employees

UCD section was just by the side of main gate in Head Office MCH and it was a common sight in the first week of every month to see few pathans waiting at the gate with their typical turbans and hand sticks to collect money from municipal employees after they receive their salaries. When a few of the debtors were asked as to what is the problem, they said "they have borrowed money ranging from 500-1000 long back and every month the pathans come to collect the interest part only keeping the capital as it is and the interest is Rs. 10 per month. Some people have paid their interest for more than 2 years without touching the capital".

The matter was discussed in house and UCD wanted to help them out. All those loanees are receiving regular salaries every month. Banks are contacted, which agreed to lend the money if the MCH directly deduct the repayment installments from their pay bills and adjust it to the banks concerned. There was positive support from the Special officer and the Examiner of Accounts also; but some employees lower down have felt as an additional burden. Still it was managed to a successful, logical end and these families were very grateful to UCD for this grand idea.

Reading Room with Old Magazines

We have about 50 reading rooms run by MCH there and the watchman there returns the old magazines soon after the receipt of the new issues. The youth in slums proposed to have read and return libraries using old magazines. The Public Relations Officer (PRO) incharge of Municipal Reading Rooms appreciated the idea and gave them the support. So at very little cost some local youth groups enjoyed reading the journals and books.

Exchange of New Textbooks for the Old

The social welfare department used to supply new textbooks every year for scheduled castes and backward class students through UCD. But we have poor students in other castes also. Not only that the number of books that the department supplies are very limited. So before giving new textbooks, the students are asked by UCD to give their textbooks of the previous class, which are in turn supplied to other students. Through this procedure, many poor students are helped in getting either new or old textbooks for the classes to which they are promoted.

Srilankan Tour

The community worker must try to kindle and keep the community's aspirations always high. This might keep him in an awkward situation at times. In early 70's a few community members predominantly women expressed their desire that they should become foreign returned at least possible expenditure (Rs. 300 in those days). Srilanka came in our minds and they all agreed. So we, the community workers could not lag behind. A tour committee was formed, money collected, itinerary fixed, correspondence initiated and the matter was stuck at passport level. How to get endorsement on so many passport applications (about 60) was a big question. If our intentions are good, we are sure to get bosses to back us up. But we must take steps to guard against future mishaps or complications.

We could find out a social work minded officer in the Secretariat and told him about the aspirations of our poor groups. He showed no hesitation to sign on the applications; but expressed the fear that these passports might be put to wrong use after the tour is completed. So we took the precaution in collecting back and bundling all the passports in our office. This was informed to the officer and he felt very happy for having given his support to the tour. There was no passport office in Hyderabad then. One of our COs has to spend few days in Madras to get these passports to the entire group.

Community Halls

Hundreds of community halls have been constructed by MCH with huge investments in 60's and 70's. After UCD came in, about 30 such halls with low investment and with humble effort of communities have come up in slums where we were working. We had the historic Telengana agitation for a separate State in 70's. Then the halls built by bureaucracy were smashed to ground. Were those that had the backing of the community and community work touched or damaged in any way? These facts should open the eyes of every one and correct the thinking of our planners and top brass to decide whether community action has to be advocated and encouraged in all earnestness or not, irrespective of the political or other affiliations.

Training in Auto-rickshaw Driving

The emphasis behind this training is : "need-orientation" and not "stipend attraction". They should be informal and of a non-institutional nature and should not disturb their normal livelihood. Things have to be adjusted accordingly. To quote an example, there were many rickshaw pullers in the project area who wanted to go in for auto-rickshaw driving which can fetch better incomes. But in 1970s there were no training centres in auto-rickshaw driving. So the rickshaw pullers have to spend all their time with an auto-rickshaw driver or a mechanic hoping that they will get training under him and this led to a lot of frustration. This was expressed as a felt need. The project approached one auto-rickshaw driver who is an office bearer in a voluntary organisation. He agreed to give training but only in the nights, outside the city. About half a dozen rickshaw pullers agreed to these conditions and the rate was negotiated at a low price. They said if this training is done in nights without any officer in the vicinity, then the police might misunderstand them and put them behind the bars. So the project had to send one organiser every night to be with them for over 15 days and spend sleepless nights.

Now the auto-rickshaw driver wanted to do the training on commercial lines. About 40 rickshaw pullers were identified and training charges and subsidy from project were decided. One municipal playground was fixed as a training place and time table was drawn out for training of rickshaw pullers. They come for training during a particular hour with their rickshaws on dot, get the training and go back to earn their livelihood. The trainer took care of obtaining temporary licences, fixing the test and finally, getting the driving licences. Now the rickshaw puller is ready to change over, hire an auto-rickshaw from some owner for a full day or part and work out his earnings.

Time was ripe after few months to organise a cooperative and go in for loans through the banks for getting auto-rickshaws of their own. So if there is the will there is a way out. How united efforts bore fruits!

At one stage, the Municipal Corporation had frozen the issue of fresh licences for rickshaws and so the old licences were changing hands at abnormal rate. An old rickshaw, with licence number, even in junk condition has greater value than a new rickshaw without licence and there were many rickshaw pullers in the project who have to pay heavy hire charge to rickshaw owners, each of whom own even one hundred rickshaws. The rickshaw pullers are eager to buy their own rickshaws, but because of the licence problem, there is no way out. The project motivated them to save about Rs. 300 as 25% margin money to get bank loan and raised a slogan on the analogy "land for tiller — rickshaw for the puller". About 400 rickshaw pullers mobilized their margin money and project could convince the municipal corporation on :

- The elimination of middlemen who give rickshaws on hire.
- Issue of licences to bonafide rickshaw pullers so that they need not go in for hired rickshaws.
- Convince banks to give loans to genuine rickshaw pullers.
- This resulted in disappearance of the premium on rickshaw licence with junk rickshaws. The rickshaw pullers diverted their daily hire charges as installment repayments and thus became the rickshaw owner, in about 10 months.

For any means of livelihood like this, which includes a sewing machine, a wet grinder, a soda making machine, a chilly powdering unit, a pop corn machine, a soap making unit, a book binding unit, a welding unit, a carpentry unit, a printing and dyeing unit, a small grocery unit, a tea shop, an egg booth, a chicken stall, a vegetable stall, a pawnshop or for anything that can attract small loans and make the beneficiaries proud earners of their livelihood, the project made its humble effort to improve their lot.

For the motivational work, the project might need a TV, a VCP or public address equipment on hire. Instead of depending upon a commercial firm, individuals or small groups in different slums are made to procure them on loan, and make a livelihood out of them. Even women started cycle taxis business, by procuring about six cycles. There are women who are supplying lunches and refreshments for functions, training camps etc., making it a remunerative activity. All these mini activities make women self-confident and are respected both in family and in community, which is only a prelude to women's empowerment and liberation.

Even with large investments, it is difficult for the bureaucracy to achieve this goal, as the element of "We and Ours" will be missing in all such deeds. If properly guided, UCD approach can derive all these results, at low cost and with utmost satisfaction.

Municipal Corporation was dissolved and the Council hall had no use. UCD with the permission from the Special Officer started using it for meetings of women and youth groups. For these groups sitting in the hall and speaking before the microphone was an unforgetable experience. But the conservatives feel it is giving them unnecessary importance.

People's Money is More Valuable

In any Government Programme, there is a preallocated budget to be spent by the officer/department concerned and utilization of that sum is his target and also his creditable achievement for review by bosses. But it is the other way round in the case of UCD where some fund is provided. But that is meant for use only when there is no one else to provide this money or to be spent only to fill in gaps. UCD aims at covering other departmental budgets to benefit its clients and at community participation, which is so valuable and absolutely possible even from the poorest and most miserable. The small coins that one scrapes from these people through persuasion and motivation is hundred times more valuable than the thousands and the lakhs that one provides in the budget.

In the old UCD project of 60s the allocation for staff salaries was Rs. 60,000 and for programmes it is only Rs. 15,000. Whenever there was a review meeting, the usual remark from the boss was "Yours is a staff oriented scheme and so the allocation will be automatically spent". But UCD is an agency with an empty pocket, but lots of programmes came up. So UCD has to motivate and tap several outside agencies to realize satisfactory results. So please tell us "Is it easy to empty ones own pocket and declare I have spent the budget" or "I have no money in my pocket, but could bring in others' cooperation and effort in different ways to materialize various things.''

7

Housing in Hyderabad — Self-Help Model

It was the brainchild of UCD in Hyderabad, drawn out of past sad experience of Government in Slum clearance programme. There were some slums in which the elders had some vision for the future and bought their dwelling sites from the landlord more as a group dealing and in exceptional cases on individual terms. But they are forbidden to construct some small pucca houses because without municipal permission they cannot do this. Municipal permission was a dream to them because the building bylaws stipulate minimum plot size and road width, which they do not have. In spite of all this, if an individual ventures to have walls and a roof over it, he does not know when it may be pulled down by the demolition squad and so there is no way out. Is there an answer to this malady? Yes, it is worked out by UCD, which paved the way for the future.

Slum Clearance

Government made huge investments with the fond hope that the poor in shacks and huts must be made to live in comfort in cement concrete houses. This was how slum clearance programme was conceived with huge investments for constructing multi-storyed tenements. The slum dweller who would be the future beneficiary to occupy one of the tenements was treated as an inert object without knowing why his old house was uprooted and when he will occupy the new tenement and under what conditions. It was mostly an engineering feat with no social dialogue between the implementing agency and the beneficiary, the only link being the contractor who undertook the work. Tenements were constructed and the municipality took its own time to give allotment letters. The local leaders are wise to have a quick buck and instigated strangers for unauthorized occupation. A few slum dwellers remained where they were under much worse living conditions than before.

Some genuine allottees have gained entry into these apartments with no stake whatsoever of their own. They have no gas stove or kerosene stove to cook food and need large volume of cheap shrub collections to act as fuel for which there is no place to keep. Some dwellers living on second floor have a rickshaw or a pushcart or goats of their own kept on the ground, which make them restless. Water and toilet problems became more acute day after day. Meanwhile the occupant is pestered by the taxman for payment of rent and there were only two alternatives left to him. At the middle of night, he removes doors and windows, which can give him paltry returns and disappear to another settlement. If he was more calculative, he looked for a customer, who was eagerly looking for a house, grab about five hundred rupees from them before handing over the position keeping the local body in complete darkness. There was continuous clamour for declaration of ownership, repairs to tenements etc., on which plea they remain as continuous defaulters to the municipality. The bureaucracy ultimately got government approval to give away the tenements on hire purchase to the actual inhabitants, who by now have become middle and lower middle income groups by mere change of hands over time.

These sad experiences made the government realize that slum clearance is not a suitable programme for slum dwellers whose habits cannot be changed overnight. Instead of conventional slums, where filth is absorbed by the mother earth, this programme created Ferro concrete-slums adding more to the health problems.

An Illustration

Devnagar is a slum, thirty years old with a single approach pathway, which is just eight feet wide, even today. There are 23 schedule caste families and this land, occupied by their huts, was purchased by the Social Welfare Department and given to them free of cost in 1971. The inhabitants were eager to have some pucca houses, with self-help effort and if possible with some external support. The Community Organizer incharge of that slum Sri D.G. Rama Rao understood their desire and to test their sincerity appraised them about the need to save some money initially. So the group decided that each family will save Rs. 500 in five months time and this was done. They approached banks for loan assistance but no bank was willing to lend them, as housing was considered a non-remunerative enterprise. However, impressed with the sincerity of this group, United Commercial bank agreed to give Rs. 1,000 to each family calling it a personal loan.

The community decided that they would have row housing in two blocks to economise on space and the expenditure on walls. The soil was loose and they wanted to go in for RCC columns. Accordingly, plans were made under guidance of Community Organizer and work started purely as a community effort and the role of UCD was to request the town planning officers not to visit this place for sometime. The columns and roofs on them were ready in a month's time; but the money was exhausted. UCD has a good rapport with NGOs and it invited a few Rotarians to visit the site and with the offer that the colony will be named as Rotary Nagar, Rs. 1,000 was sanctioned as assistance for each unit from the Rotary Club and with this, bricks, mud walls and doors and windows were fixed. Now UCD has something to show to its own bosses. They came and realized that these beautiful houses were the result of the initiative and participation from the people and everything is possible even in a slum situation. The plot size is hardly 200 sq. ft. with 10 ft. wide roads, which are far below the building rules. Impressed with the enthusiasm of the slum people, the Special Officer sanctioned Rs. 500 to each house as grant for purchase of cement and sand to complete plastering and flooring. With this multiple support from various sources they all have a clean place to live. Further developments, over and above this, depended on individual capacity, capability and determination.

Now, the community is proud of their team effort and very grateful to the UCD for the innovative support. Most of the group meetings were held at nights and on holidays. There was no direction from outside and it was purely an instinct from within UCD. With this sort of collaboration, the project could initiate three more housing experiments, *viz.*, Jayceenagar, Rotary Basti and Lions Nagar in over one year's time. They proved to be the cornerstones for the subsequent massive Habitat Housing Programme aiming at 13,000 houses.

The following observations were made evident through this experiment :

1. The Government and municipality realised that the building rules need drastic amendments to suit to the slum conditions and UCD was advised to continue the task and obtain amendments from Government wherever needed. But a day has come, with massive programme expansion and proposals for relaxation pouring in, the governement said "relaxation in building rules are permitted to be made by the UCD project itself with prior permission of municipal commissioner as far as habitat slums are concerned". This is an illustration that shows the confidence that is reposed on the project by the government.
2. Housing agencies, specially meant for the task, could hardly construct 5,000 houses in two decades time. How is it possible for UCD to construct 13,000 houses was a big question. The answer was that "UCD was not constructing 13,000 houses. There are 13,000 families to do their own housing". UCD is just a facilitator.
3. To improve slum conditions, housing and environment have to be intensified and should go hand in hand. The Government realised this and enabled identification of 13,000 house sites in different slums whose titles for ownership were given to the occupants in the joint names of husband and wife, using UCD as an effective liaison and link. Government also ordered that environmental improvement had to be taken up first in slums where housing is started.
4. A socio-economic survey was undertaken by UCD in all slums and the list of dwellers in each slum was made out in advance. Then it was made clear to the people there, that the whole piece of land will be theirs as a group and if they allow others to come and settle afresh, that would

cut down their plot size. This was to curtail further immigration to limit the density of slum to its old status.

5. Using fixed term deposits as a bait, the Municipal Corporation could influence several banks in the city to extend loan facility for self-help housing at Rs. 4,000 per Unit. Nobody bothered about it, as it was a small individual loan.

   But at one stage, the Reserve Bank noted with surprise that nearly 40 million rupees were advanced for housing in Hyderabad alone which was against the Bank policy, as housing is considered a non-remunerative investment. So a high-level banking team arrived in Hyderabad, to find out the reasons. UCD could convince them that self-help housing loan for the poor in slums is not a non-remunerative investment by showing what was the situation of the slum dweller earlier when compared to what he is today. In the old shack or hut, he has no security and no urge for betterment. He is content with mud utensils, ragged mats, children with torn clothes and his age-old habits to forget his misery temporarily. When he enters his new home created out of his sweat and toil with Bank loan support, his priorities and urges are completely changed. He wishes to have cots in place of mats, electric bulb in place of lamp with soot, stainless steel utensils and clean dresses for him and his children. He does not like his children to loiter on roads and he wants them to go to school. When asked what about his old liquor addiction he retorted with no hesitation "where is the money and time to think about all that." The bank team thus was fully convinced of the social and behavioural change that this housing activity was creating. All their doubts are cleared and they also felt that the individual loan amount should be increased to Rs. 6,000 per unit and also agreed to sanction Rs. 1,000 as extra loan to pursue some avocation for additional income generation which would enable him to pay the loan instalments regularly.

6. At one stage, the Government agreed to give Rs. 1,000 as subsidy to each house, if housing is to be undertaken by UCD or some other agency direct but the subsidy was found unfeasible for self-help housing. But the beneficiary felt that he will do his own housing even if there is no subsidy. He can use his old housing material and put in his own effort to make it cheaper and stronger. This gave a great relief to the agency because he is constructing his own house and UCD is releasing instalments according to progress of work shown. There was heavy rain one night and because of that one wall of a particular house in a slum had collapsed. The next day when the project staff visited the site and asked why it happened, the reply was completely different and beyond the imagination of a bureaucrat. He said it was due to a construction mistake and that he would rectify it immediately. So which is better? Is it beneficiary involved activity or agency implemented activity? The bureaucracy can enjoy great relief, if it is to be the former approach but how is it they do not like it and still opt for receiving criticism and cudgels from people, who are on the offensive and very critical against bureaucratic attitude.

Road No. 12 Experience

At times the project was forced to push the community fast to derive quick decision from them because of official pressures from above. But the community was not ready to act fast and there was a gap, which at times caused misunderstanding or even antogonism. A field narration to corroborate this type of experience is :

There was a slum at the entrance of *Road No. 12, Banjara Hills* with over 200 families consisting of Vadders and Erukalas belonging to schedule tribes. In the same Road No. 12, top officials in government and business magnates also live and they all somehow wanted to evict these families and rehabilitate them somewhere else. This is because there were constant quarrels and outbursts amongst the slum people due to their own addictions common to the working class and which created unpleasant scenes in the evening hours. The Government also identified an alternate place for their rehabilitation nearby but then came the vehement resistance from the people. This task was entrusted to UCD, which made lot of efforts for over two months to motivate and convince them. The resistance from their side grew stronger and stronger and ultimately the project has thought of alternate strategy in the meeting of Director with staff. None of the project staff visited that community for the next two months. One evening the community leaders in the slum were informed that the project staff is coming for an informal get together wherein everybody would get their own food, dine together and then sing some bhajans.

Before actually attempting this, there was a funny idea from some of our colleagues, which was like this : ''Let us all go there and stay till every one sleeps. Then we go home and come back again before the first person in the slum gets up". They did not understand how suicidal it is for a community worker.

The community made arrangements and the event went off merrily with the participation of some of the elite from Road No. 12 also.

It was decided that the Director and some of the project staff will sleep for the night in the slum itself accepting the facilities that are available and offered by the community leaders. The people were very happy with the night's get together and the stay of project staff was in the thatched school shed, which was half-open to sky. Leaders said they are unhappy with the condition of the school shed and they could have repaired it much earlier.

Ten days later three leaders came from the slum and said "you gave us some advice regarding our security of stay by rehabilitation to some other site nearby and we want to see that place before a final decision is taken by all of us". Then again persuasion process started and within two months the entire community moved to the plots at the new site and pitched their huts which ultimately developed into a nice housing colony.

Before taking up the project, the top officials in the Corporation assured that the whole area from where the slum will be evicted will be converted into a park and the government will also construct a small community hall for use by that community. That never happened and a big multi-storeyed complex has come there. That was a matter of great disappointment for the project and the community and it is one's own guess who benefited most from this deal.

The Community Development Process in Self-help Housing in Fateh Sultan Lane — A Case Study

This case illustrates a number of important things about the community development process in a self-help housing project. It emphasizes the importance of skilled, sensitive, patient community workers and the time-consuming nature of conflict resolution and consensus building which are central to the genuine process. It also is a lively example of how the creativity of people themselves can solve problems which have baffled the professional community development workers.

Fateh Sultan Lane is a community of 142 families which had been in existence for more than 20 years. It was in a congested area of the central city where the members were squatting on some very valuable land of about 1.6 acres. The social welfare department gave pattas to the residents there. But the extent of each patta varied from 10 to 60 sq. yds. depending upon the position one was enjoying at that time.

In 1976 the state government had decided to give "pattas" (deeds) to 13,000 slum families who were living in "unobjectionable slums", which means slums located on public land, not designated for some other important purposes. The Hyderabad Urban Community Development project, under the Municipal Corporation, had been given the task of stimulating and overseeing the construction of self-help housing in the selected communities where pattas had been awarded. This is instead of following the usual government practice of constructing multi-storeyed tenements under slum clearance programme.

The project took its usual community development approach and arranged with some banks to give loans to families with pattas at a low rate of interest of 4% p.a. (differential rate of interest). Each family was to contribute 20% of the cost of the house in cash, kind, labour and/or supervision. The bank loan would cover the other 80%. At the beginning of the project, the total estimated cost of one of these small houses on a plot of approximately 30 sq. mtrs. was Rs. 5,000. The project established the following ground rules : A community could be considered for this self-help housing assistance if it first agreed to pull down all its existing houses and allow the town planning wing of the project to develop an orderly layout with streets, lanes and housing plots. Each of these plot owners have to agree — his plot would be of equal size; no matter what the variation in size of the present holdings of the community members might be. The project was committed not to disrupt the existing spatial relations among members of the community. If I had lived next to Mr. A, I should continue to do so in the new lay-out.

Fateh Sultan Lane community did not come in the UCD project area. But some local enthusiastic residents had requested that it be taken up under the Habitat scheme. Since it was decided that each plot should be approximately 40 sq. yds., they soon realized that it would be impossible to accommodate all 142 families in the area occupied by the old community. Innumerable discussions took place and it took four months before the problems could be resolved successfully. Even then the solution came from the people themselves, rather than from the project staff. Since no one wanted to move, one day some of the people asked "Why not have two-storeyed buildings?" This was a startling idea since single-storeyed houses had been the regular pattern in the other communities taken up and besides, as one project staff member put it "How could this be done since each family had a patta?'' ''It is easy", replied the community members, "One family with a patta would live downstairs and one family with same patta would live upstairs". The project staff realized that the idea was a good one but at this time there was no law in Hyderabad allowing people to have ownership flats : so they decided to overcome this problem by different numbering system. They would simply number the downstairs flat as No. 1 and the upstairs plot as 1A and so on. The people also had some interesting ideas about design and where the stairways would be.

The problem did not end here. There were a series of extended negotiations about who would live upstairs and who would live downstairs. Finally, a set of criteria and a list of priority persons was worked out by the community organizer, based on the length of stay of individual families and the size of the plot one owned earlier. In the layout, one side of the lane had single storey houses and the other side had double-storey houses to accommodate all families.

By these criteria, the question of who would live in the single-storey house, who would live downstairs in the double-storey houses, who would live upstairs in the double-storey houses, and who would live next to whom and who would live above whom, all had been worked out.

A third problem which arose was that some residents had moved elsewhere and they decided to return and take advantage of the opportunity of getting a brick and mortar house with a secured right to the land. Again, the community organizers and the community leaders had to meet together and draw up a list of people who were legitimate residents of Fateh Sultan Lane.

At last all of these problems were sorted out through this often frustrating but persistent process of dialogue among community members with the community organizers. It was a tedious and difficult process of consensus building but finally all problems were resolved and construction took place.

Lessons from Fateh Sultan Lane are the following :

Given the chance people will often find creative solutions to the problems which face them. The process of decision-making and consensus building in a community often is an extremely time-consuming one which requires great openness, patience and skill and a fundamental belief about the ability of poor people to participate in decisions which affect themselves.

The participatory approach to housing leads to results which go far beyond the physical house. As in the case of Fateh Sultan Lane, it is an educative and community-building exercise which has relevance long after the actual construction has taken place. We do not have any data on how many houses have been sold off by the original owners in Fateh Sultan Lane but one would be inclined to believe that after this experience, the houses would not be perceived as simply commodities by their builders. On the other hand, houses which are constructed and supplied by housing authorities in an arbitrary way with no participation or very little participation by the residents are likely to be perceived in a very different manner.

Shelter as a Means of Social Change

Improvement of Shelter under Urban Community Development Programme linked to the norm is only one of the means of social change and therefore self-help housing is introduced for the slum communities. Under this process the individual family and the group involves fully and learns the banking building material cost and procurement rules, market trends, selectivity, substitutes, economy and thrift. The involvement of the people as individual families is total. The proposed layout pattern, extent of plot area, the road pattern, location of the open spaces, identifying of the target group with individual plot, the design for the house-keeping in view, the predominant occupation and the size of the family are not only designed in consultation with the slum communities, but they are explained fully the programmes, the constraints and the liability of burden, the advantages and disadvantages and the slum community is prepared after series of meetings with the representatives from the families directly as a result of which the self-help housing programmes may look slower in accomplishing targets, but are qualitative and acceptable to the community. The goals achieved are perceptible and social changes are seen in these communities.

As the then Special Officer of Municipal Corporation of Hyderabad, Sri N. Luther has opined, the housing problems of the poor could be tackled with more cost efficiency through individual rather than organisational effort, which would normally multiply the cost and still not ensure quality.

✪

8

Gyanajyoti Mahila Mandali — A Case Study

It came into existence in 1968 with the following aims :

(1) To educate the women and children.

(2) To provide leisure time activities and

(3) To organize and participate in cultural and recreational activities.

Towards fulfilment of its first aim, the Mahila Mandali started a Balwadi which was inaugurated as "Netaji Balwadi" on 27-2-1969 with 30 children, by the then Mayor of the Municipal Corporation of Hyderabad, Smt. Kumud B. Naik. The Balwadi was located in the Municipal Community Hall in Fatehulla Baig Lane near Charminar. Smt. Laxmi Narsamma, an old lady of about 60 years and founder member of the Mahila Mandali donated an amount of Rs. 25 to the Balwadi.

The families from which the Balwadi children were enrolled were poor and the UCD Programme is based on the twin norms of self-help and people's participation. Collection of a monthly fee of Re. 1 for each child attending the Balwadi was considered important and necessary.

The amount was utilized for purchase of equipment, organizing competitions among children, National Days, Festivals etc., with matching aid from the Urban Community Development Project. Subsequently the fee was enhanced to Rs. 3 in 1973 and it was further enhanced subsequently. Very soon the strength was increased to 50 and two teachers were engaged to manage the Balwadi.

Impact on Parents

This collection of one rupee every month from each child made the parents to think about the services rendered to the children in the Balwadi, about the utilisation of the amount by the Mahila Mandali and about the progress of learning by the children.

Every month when they came into contact with the Balwadi teacher or the Secretary of the Mahila Mandali for payment of the fee, they used to enquire about their child's progress. They also offered suggestions for change or improvement which in turn made the UCD as well as the Mahila Mandali to consider the necessity and usefulness of introducing the system of parents-meetings periodically to review working of the institution and discuss problems and suggestions for improvement. This type of interaction developed a sort of partnership between the parents and the Balwadi on one side and between the parents and the Mahila Mandali on the other. This helped the parents to keep the children neat and tidy, give coaching at home, watch the progress made, teach poems and songs, take health care and nutrition etc., while for the teacher it was easy to communicate with the parents about the deficiencies in the child, steps to be taken to improve and so on.

The parents meetings not only formed a forum for review of Balwadi activity, but also promoted collective thinking on various matters of common interest like area problems, sanitation condition, social get-togethers, cooking demonstrations, film shows, home keeping, baby shows, immunization of children, nutrition etc.

For the UCD project the rupee one paid by the parent of the child brought out many lessons. There is perceptible change in the face of the child and also the mother. To a query the mother says, she was paying rupee one from her hard earned money for the child. She admitted that the boy learnt some rhymes, behaving in a disciplined manner and was comparatively cleaner. She also complained that the teacher insisted on having neat clothes which she could not afford. She also later revealed that her two other children were also changing because of this boy. It is a great contrast to another family which was not paying any money for her child going to a Balwadi. The mother was found indifferent to the changing conditions of the boy. Her total approach was entirely different.

Impact on Mahila Mandali

The meager amount collected every month was not sufficient to meet the requirements of the Balwadi like equipment, services of ayah and other miscellaneous charges. This compelled the members to think ways and means of enhancing the resources. The involvement of parents in the Balwadi activity has necessitated the Mahila Mandali to maintain good standards, efficient teachers and proper equipment.

To meet the increasing responsibilities, the Mahila Mandali experimented various measures to improve its financial status under supervision and guidance of the UCD Community Organizer. A mini lottery was conducted, film shows were organized, different recipes were prepared and sold among members present during cooking demonstrations, condiments like chilly powder, turmeric powder, papad, badaya etc. were prepared and sold to business establishments, hotels, private houses etc., study tours and picnics organized on cost sharing basis and the profits derived from all these activities were credited to the Mahila Mandali fund. The donations and contributions that were collected during National Days and festivals, Bhajan programmes etc. and the savings were added to the Mahila Mandali funds. The Mahila Mandali could, thus raise its deposits to about Rs. 7,000 within a short period of 4-5 years excluding the cost of Balwadi maintenance.

The one rupee fee collection has not only made the Mahila Mandali to raise funds for the Balwadi, but was also responsible for introducing varied nature of activities for the benefit of local women and children, by which the Mahila Mandali had become popular in the entire locality of about 500 families and has grown as an active organization in the Urban Community Development Project.

Thus the one rupee Balwadi fee has established strong links between parent-teacher relations, teacher-pupil relations and parent-welfare organization relations and has contributed for the growth of local activity from a small Balwadi to a multi-phased development of the locality.

9

Community Development Activities in a Nutshell

The project identified in course of time many items falling under several groups like water, sanitation, health, nutrition, education, economic improvement, community organization, training, strengthening of voluntary organizations, social, cultural and recreational activities.

Education

1. Balwadies.
2. Anganwadies
3. Adult Literacy Centres
4. Coaching Centres
5. Creche Centres

Social

1. Dance Centres
2. Self-help Reading Room & Libraries
3. Study Tours
4. Get-togethers
5. Film Shows
6. Seminars
7. Symposia
8. Exhibitions
9. Social Get-togethers
10. Condensed Courses for School Dropouts

11. Exchange of Textbooks
12. Supply of Dresses to Poor Students
13. Radio Programmes
14. Supply of T.Vs
15. Simple marriages
16. Intercaste marriages
17. Exchange visits
18. Rotary books
19. Social welfare dresses

Food and Nutrition

1. Cooking Demonstrations
2. Food Preservation Classes

Recreation

1. Sports & Games Competitions
2. Melas & Festivals
3. Song & Drama Programmes
4. Quawalies
5. Mushaira
6. Kavisammelans
7. Bhajans
8. Burra Kathas
9. Hari Kathas
10. Basti Welfare Committees
11. Youth Organizations
12. Mahila Mandals
13. Children Organizations
14. Bhajan Mandals
15. Leadership Camps
16. Field Orientation in UCD

Training

1. Sewing Centres

2. Zig Zag Centres
3. Doll Making
4. Type/Shorthand Centres
5. Motor Car Driving Courses
6. Auto-Rickshaw Driving Courses
7. Radio Mechanism Courses
8. T.V. Repairing
9. Photography Courses
10. Computer Punching Courses
11. Air Conditioning & Refrigeration
12. Fabric Painting
13. Sewing Machine Repairs
14. Repairs of Electrical Appliances
15. Plumbing and Wiring
16. Masonry
17. Prefab Cement Products
18. Tiles Laying & Flooring
19. Secretarial & Receptionist Courses
20. Composing & Printing
21. Motor Winding

Economic

1. Training for office bearers of Mahila Mandals
2. Physical Education Classes
3. Sewing Machine Loans
4. Cycle Rickshaw Loans
5. Loans to Petty Vendors
6. Garment Making
7. Lijjat Papad
8. Supporting Mahila Mandal Activities
9. Card Board Units
10. Cycle Rickshaw Co-operatives

11. Carpenters Co-operatives
12. Blacksmiths
13. Tailoring Co-operatives
14. Charmakara Sangams
15. Aid from Voluntary Organizations
16. Supply of Machines at concessional rates

Health

1. Health Checkup Camps
2. Eye Camps
3. Supply of Spectacles
4. Immunization Camps
5. Balwadi Health Checkup
6. Integrated Health Care Centres
7. Dental Checkup Programmes
8. Massive Dose of Vitamin 'A'
9. Malaria Depots
10. SNP Centres
11. Family Welfare Activities
12. Propaganda Meetings
13. Vasectomy Operations
14. Tubectomy/Laproscopic Operations
15. Sanitary Drives
16. Mass Deworming for Children

Housing

1. Distribution of house site pattas
2. No. of slums taken-up under Habitat housing
3. No. of houses constructed by Bank Loans
4. No. of houses constructed with HUDCO assistance

Sanitation

1. Water closets provided
2. Toilets constructed

3. No. of Slums provided with Basic civic amenities
4. Self-help Community halls constructed
5. Community halls constructed in collaboration with other agencies
6. Tree Plantation
7. Fruit Trees planted
8. New drains constructed
9. Old drains repaired
10. Soak pits constructed
11. Sanitation drives organized
12. New water stand posts
13. Water pipelines laid
14. Tube-wells installed
15. Tube-wells cleaned
16. Wells cleaned
17. Platforms around tube-wells
18. Platforms around stand posts
19. Street lights provided
20. Ventilators supplied
21. Community pials constructed

10

UCD Contribution to the Situation of Women and Children

1. The Home Situation

- Where people have been involved, public facilities such as water taps, dust-bins and drains are better maintained by the community.
- Self-help houses are much better maintained, less likely to be sold and loans are more likely to be repaid.
- Pre-primary schools give time to free mothers for other work.

2. Health Status

- Credibility of project staff persuades people to participate in immunization drives and to bring children for regular medical check-ups. And over time, results convince people about the efficacy of such measures in controlling disease and preventing illness and more use is made of available health facilities.

3. Literacy Status

- Women begin attending literacy classes often because of faith in project staff, they will continue to do so only if the classes give them something they need; how to keep accounts, how to fill a form for a loan, etc.
- Coaching classes help poor children to keep up with lessons where illiterate parents cannot help them.

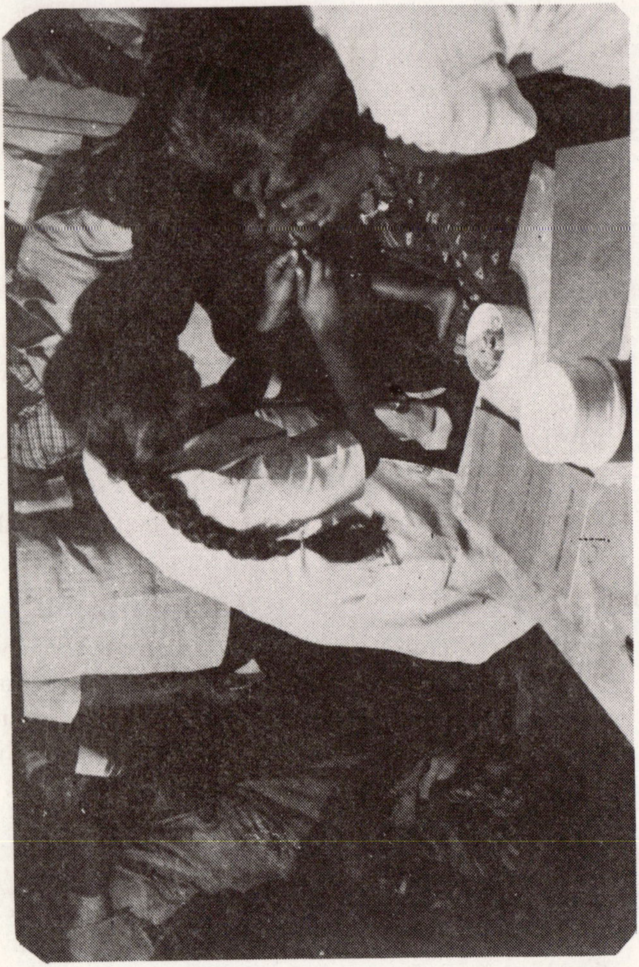

UNIVERSAL IMMUNISATION PROGRAMME FOR CHILDREN

4. Economic Status

- Sewing classes and sewing machines on a hire purchase basis are in great demand.
- Training in skills for income-generation.
- The need for extra income leads to community involvement and involvement to the continuity of an activity.

5. Increasing Awareness

- Involvement in community activities enhances confidence and awareness and widens the horizons of poor women and children.

✪

11

Baseline, Monitoring and Review

Base Line

On 10 per cent families, socio-economic survey was conducted in the original project to acquaint COs with the baseline situation, to understand the communities, its leader, its way of functioning, existing conditions and the level of their awareness. It also simultaneously helped the project to introduce the programme and the project objectives to the people. A pamphlet also was passed on during family contacts, giving information about the project. The title of the pamphlet was "*UCD pilot project — a people's programme in Ward No. 22*".

The process of survey generated spontaneous response from the people and their readiness to involve in the project work straightaway opened up a stream of activities, small and big.

The data in the family contact cards of this baseline survey was also made use of as part of the study by Dr. William J. Cousins and Catherine Guider, in their book *Changing Slum Communities*.

Block Maps

Detailed block maps were prepared by the COs in their respective areas by means of which the location of a house in the project area can be found out with the help of house numbers.

Slum Surveys

In 1974, an exhaustive survey was undertaken by the project for all the slums in the city with the assistance of a small team of investigators. This was to formulae the "programme for Integrated Services for youth and children in the city of Hyderabad".

An officers committee was constituted by the Government with the representatives of Revenue, Town planning and Social Welfare department with Commissioner, MCH as the Chairman and the Director, UCD as convenor. This committee identified 672 slums with a population of 8.20 lakhs in municipal corporation limits in 1987. Based on this data, master plans I, II, III for slum improvement were developed for ODA assistance. The data has proved very useful in developing subsequent schemes.

The project staff periodically undertook survey in the city to identify slums and slum population for various services like issue of house site pattas, Habitat scheme, environmental upgradation programmes, etc. In collaboration with the town planning and revenue departments UCD conducted physical and socio-economic survey of all 484 slums identified by the cabinet sub-committee for issue of house site pattas (title deeds).

As a follow up to the interactions with other departments and voluntary agencies, a general survey of slums was done, with the intention of creating a database. This survey was conducted in 1987 utilizing the services of NSS volunteers.

Monitoring and Review

Normally, the project staff used to work in the field in the forenoon and in offices in the afternoon. Sundays and holidays were their real active days in the field. Night halts in slums had long lasting impact. The staff, in addition to informal sharing of experiences daily, used to have staff meetings once in a week chaired by the project officer. These staff meetings constituted the most effective planning, monitoring and review sessions. The dynamic and democratic leadership and commitment and team spirit of the project staff were responsible for the rapid strides, the project made in the direction of progress carrying the people with it. The project was run under the overall control of Commissioner/ Special Officer of the Municipal Corporation. Joint inspections by the municipal commissioner and other heads of departments to the projects, corporation level review meetings, and visits of Secretaries to Government to the project areas, occasional meetings at the secretariat — all helped as means of review and monitoring of the programme.

Evaluation

The programme was evaluated first in the early 1970s by Dr. Subash Chandra and Dr. S.P. Punelekar, *vide* the publication "UCD Programme in India" by the National Institute of Public Cooperation and Child Development, New Delhi.

Several studies on UCD Hyderabad were made by a number of people pursue their Ph.D. Students of social work and housing and architecture from Andhra Pradesh and outside used to come for block placement.

MACONS did an evaluation of UCD in early 80, supported by UNICEF. Under ODA, U.K. assisted slum improvement project; an evaluation was conducted by the centre for development studies, Swansea University, U.K. and the Council for Social Development, Hyderabad in the latter part of 1980s.

12

Degree of Participation and Interaction

The Basti welfare committees, youth clubs, mahila mandals, interest groups, etc., were the backbones of the project. In each slum/locality the existing association and leadership were identified. The project worked with them to promote their interests and objectives. At the same time, new ideas were generated for further development.

Number of self-help community halls were built and existing community centers were improved, for introducing several activities like balwadies, sewing centers. 50% matching grants were provided by the project against the contributions raised by the people in cash, kind and labour, *e.g.*

- For community halls, if the walls are raised upto roof levels, roofing material was supplied by the project.
- Whenever a youth rally/children's rally/women's rally was organized, the representatives of the community organizations did the whole planning. They formed into organization committees and shouldered entire responsibility for conducting it.
- Similarly, for starting a balwadi / sewing centre, in addition to providing accommodation freely, the people took responsibility for managing and developing the centres themselves. Project sanctioned teacher's honorarium and only 50% matching grant for teaching aids. In all the activities people played the major role, whereas the project provided the needed succour directly or indirectly through its liaison role.

- For creating awareness and to bring the services down to the slum areas, symposia were conducted in the localities to which the officials were invited. The people made local arrangements themselves. Thereby people's needs and their organization's role were understood by the officials of the Government and municipal departments *e.g.* Health, Industry, etc. Thereafter, people approached them directly to get benefit of their services, without the liaison of the project staff.
- Local voluntary service organizations like Rotary, Lions, Jaycees, YMCA gave much support to the programme. They helped in house-improvement, self-help housing colonies *e.g.* Rotary Basti, Rotary Nagar, East Lions Nagar, Jaycees Nagar, etc.
- Lions club under their sight conservation programme conducted a number of eye camps in the project areas through the project. The Nizam's charitable Trust was associated with the project by sanctioning grants for spectacles, etc.

Impact of the Interactions

Few examples are given hereunder :

- People could get clean drinking water by additional taps, handpumps. Slum dwellers got public latrines within their slums. In one slum, the community members bought a piece of land and the MCH constructed latrines for men, women and children separately. Special washing platforms were constructed and used, in certain localities thereby improving the sanitation.
- Activities like clean house competitions, baby shows, sanitation drives, construction of small drains on self-help basis by the slum dwellers, community halls, health checkups, eye camps, etc., created civic consciousness and healthy living.
- The balwadies, study tours, radios, matriculation coaching centres in the slums paved the way for and opened the doors of education to the children as otherwise the children would never have gone to normal schools. The

performance of the balwadi children was better than others in the 1st standard.

- There is better awareness among mothers about education, health, sanitation, nutrition, etc.
- By means of sewing centres, many learnt tailoring and they started garments manufacturing units.
- Lijjat papad cottage industry started in 1970s is a shining example of the development of women, which is managed by women only and now over 200 women are earning about Rs. 900 per month regularly.

Lessons Learnt

1. Political will at Government and local body level is necessary to launch programmes for urban poor directed at community development.
2. Community development approach is reinforced by conviction on the part of bureaucrats.
3. Identification and study of voluntary and independent experiments in community participation in different parts of the country helped in developing a realistic and workable strategy for community involvement, in conformity with local traditions.
4. Attachment of UCD projects as a part of Municipal Corporation had many advantages and facilitated fast enlargement of the programme.
5. Committed staff with right attitude and understanding of the programme goals is an asset.
6. Selection of right type of field staff is very vital; suitable persons are to be identified by the project, if necessary, by amending the established recruitment procedures.
7. Humble beginning with simple activities and gradual realization of their own capacities by the communities *e.g.* start with cleaning wells, formation of drains, starting of balwadies, construction of community halls, housing, environmental upgradation and integrated development.
8. Activities entirely based on the felt needs of the people are very satisfying and generate maximum participation.

9. Local basti level community organizations are the backbone of the projects, they have to be identified / started and strengthened with supporting activities.
10. Voluntary workers are to be engaged by the community organizations instead of by the project/municipal authorities; the grants may be passed on from the project to the organization.
11. Base line survey not by outsiders and specially engaged staff but by community and the community organizers served as a good foundation for the project (Community Self Survey).
12. Women derived overwhelming exposure in the development process and they evolved number of activities with little motivation.
13. Neighbourhood development committee approach and empowering people is the key to successful mobilization.
14. Limited funding resulted in more emphasis on people's participation and for designing low cost activities.
15. Doling out funds from outside may seriously damage the community participation and development process, if the outlook and goal is only for absorption of funds.
16. Establish linkages between project and other departments and voluntary agencies, ultimately between them and people. Flexibility in project management methods is obviously very important to sustain people's interest.
17. Security of tenure (house site ownership) is a great incentive for participatory process of community development in slums.
18. Self-help housing is a potential entry point for community development. It attracted good response from the people.
19. The under current of people's participation in all activities should be maintained scrupulously — activities were used as a means to community development.
20. The first project should be for demonstration. Teamwork of the project staff, carrying the people with them is the basic need for a meaningful programme.

21. Working with people during their convenient hours and on their weekly holidays must be acceptable to the field workers.
22. Several funding agencies, other departments, voluntary organizations, banks, and even International agencies will come forward to associate themselves with the project, when once the usefulness, the strong community-base of the project and its popularity are well established.
23. New projects have to be introduced/extended where urge is expressed by the people, like readiness to fully involve in this people's participatory programme.
24. Experienced staff of initial project should move to newly started project for successful replication.
25. The project established an image of non-political nature and a solely development concern. This is how UCD got equally good appreciation from corporators belonging to all political parties.
26. In addition to field apprenticeship under senior project staff, emphasis should be laid on periodical training of functionaries at regular intervals.

✪

13

Decline in Community Participation

(a) Till about 1980, the status and image of UCD was very encouraging and the workers have succeeded in reaching all the slum families. They adapted innovative techniques and methods to solve local problems. UCD generated lot of hope and enthusiasm amongst slum communities and proved that organised efforts can improve social and economic conditions at low cost.

UCD proved that slum is not just the outcome of physical factors. Slum improvement has to be tackled in an integrated way.

Self-help and people's participation strengthened the ideas that process is more important than end product. This principle was the one that acted as foundation for UCD in Hyderabad.

UCD has not only aimed at an improved slum but it taught the communities the methods of solving their own problems. Capable leadership was built up and the hitherto hopeless slum dwellers are now full of hope and confidence. The role of UCD was to build up the capacity of slum dwellers, to generate local initiative and to involve slum communities in planning and execution.

(b) Three types of community halls have come up. In the first type, the community's participation was insisted upon. In these self-help types of community halls, the people had to construct the wall upto the roof level. The UCD department gave funds for laying the roof, 50% being given by the UNICEF and another 50% by the Municipal Corporation. In the second variety, the Municipal Corporation itself had the halls constructed. There was no people's involvement. But the hall was made available for their use. The third variety are those constructed with the assistance of the Overseas Development Administration. Here again, the people's involvement is not there. Thus, there has been a steady decline of people's participation in the construction of the physical amenities. Human development, through participation, is the aim of the project. But that is being neglected. As one official put it "there has been dilution of the original objectives."

(c) Physical improvement in cooperation with the people will lead to their development also. "The departure of the UNICEF from the scene has coincided with the start of the decline in people's participation" : observed one official. The improvement of the conditions of women, especially, has declined. Not many schemes have been introduced to enable them to increase the family income. For the total development of the slums, besides the physical infrastructure, human development must also be taken up.

(d) It was with great regret that one learnt that two community halls constructed some years ago were encroached upon and sold away by the Basti leaders in one slum. The Community halls were constructed along with the houses for residents under the Habitat Programme nearly a decade ago. An engineering Company has constructed another for the use of the community.

(e) A Municipal employee, Mr. Shaik Imam, recounted how a training class to teach people to make file tags had to be closed after it had functioned for nearly a year. Bombs were hurled into the building, housing the training camp. A few people had objected to the continuance of the training class, complaining about noise pollution. Mr. Imam lamented that women who were earning anything from Rs. 300 to Rs. 600 a month had lost their source of income. His own daughter was earning Rs. 300. She was not having any income now.

(f) Five hundred and fifty houses were constructed in Mahatma Gandhi Nagar and nearby Indiranagar. Seventy-five per cent of the people for whom the houses were constructed had sold them away and shifted to other slums.

(g) It is interesting to note that originally in one slum only nine of the allottees were Muslims. Now this community owns 75% of the houses. Each house has been constructed on a plot measuring 40 sq. yds.

(h) The contribution made by UNICEF can never be forgotten. For seven years it provided, on an average, Rs. 10 lakhs per year. The UNICEF opted out of the project when it was confident that the slum dwellers would be able to mend their own fences. It had brought about tremendous awareness among the people. The UNICEF realised that no real development was possible until the women and children of the slum were taken care of and their situation improved.

(i) The Overseas Development Administration's assistancc to develop 210 slums in the first and 300 in the second year of its involvement (during the second and third phase of the Slum Improvement Project in the city) seeks to provide civic infrastructures. An official of the UCD department confessed that the Department did not have the UNICEF's concept of Neighbourhood Committees. Unlike the Neighbourhood Committees, which are all women organizations, the Basti (locality) Welfare Committees have predominantly male leadership. They easily silence the women members or push them into the background. Exclusive women's organisations, Mahila Mandalis were formed in some areas but the president of such Mandalis played a dominating role.

✪

14

UCD and UNICEF

This is a maiden attempt introducing Hyderabad Urban Community Development Project, which attempts to improve the living conditions of the people in the backward areas of the City through a process of self-help.

(a) The project started in the year 1967 aims at creating a sense of Social Coherence on Neighbourhood basis, developing a sense of belonging to the Urban Community in every family, bringing about a change in attitudes, developing local initiative and ensuring fuller utilization of the technical and welfare services through self-help. Towards this end, the project has been developing various methodologies normally employed in social planning such as corporate civic action, promoting National Integration, concentrating on people's initiative, organization, self-help and mutual aid. Since the project is an integral part of Municipal Corporation, its emphasis is also on creating civic consciousness and motivating people to improve their conditions of their lives.

(b) Women and children's programmes assumed greater importance with the association of UNICEF in 1977. The urban planners — particularly the Social Planners world over have been evincing interest in this project. Although the assistance of the UNICEF is only about a million rupees per annum and the cost of services including the physical and social development runs to 10 to 15 times the assistance, the association of UNICEF by itself is of a greater value in terms of expert advice, guidance and message on Women and Children's Health etc. The project by itself, which was covering only 20% of the backward population prior to

1977, multiplied by geometrical progression since UNICEF association in 1977, expanding from 3 projects to 12 projects.

(c) 15 years working of this project has lent concrete evidence that the Social and Environmental changes in Urban Communities can be brought about fast only by intelligent harnessing and utilization of the immense potentialities of the people. It has also vouched to the fact that social adaptation and community integration is much more relevant in the urban areas than in the Rural. This Organization has been producing a change not only in physical environment but also in the man's conduct and behaviour. Hence the problems of urban community are far more in number than those of the Rural. The political and social change and tensions of urban life are bound to stall the process of urban development if they are not controlled. It will therefore be the primary task of the UCD programme to watch and study these trends and to direct the various forces into useful constructive channels. The programme should therefore be a continuous and an all time process.

15

Trends in Urban Community Development in India

Dr. William J. Cousins, UNICEF Advisor on Urban Development in India was a source of inspiration in 1980's and early 90's and his advice and guidance went a long way in carving Hyderabad UCD. Some of his personal views and reflections about UCD are given below :

What is Community Development?

Community Development is a process through which people undertake to improve the quality of life in their community through their own cooperative thought and action. From the beginning the key concepts have been "self-help" and "felt needs." These imply that the members of the community attempt to address the needs, which they feel and perceive through their own collective efforts in the first instance. It is only when the meeting of these needs calls for resources beyond their immediate capacity that they seek additional resources from outside the community; whether it be from government or other sources.

Outside Incentives

We often assume that it is necessary to give people material "incentives" in order to get them to do something useful about their problems. This seems both patronizing and manipulative to me. It certainly does not imply much respect for the people, or for their intelligence. But, on the other hand, it is likely to "work in the short run'' : that is, people are likely to exhibit the desired behaviour : whether it is transplanting paddy in lines or accepting a family planning method. In the long run, however, incentives may always be required in order to repeat this behaviour. It is well to bear in mind a Tamil proverb, which goes : "If you mention money, even a corpse will open its mouth." The Persian equivalent may be even more appropriate in terms of effecting behaviour : "If the rope is free, I will hang myself." In short, the incentives may bring about temporary behavioural change, but it is questionable whether a self-perpetuating developmental process has been commenced. Further, the next time a problem arises, people may wait for the appearance of an "incentive" before taking "self-help" action. This seems to be development in reverse or "undevelopment."

Two Basic Assumptions

Every person has a brain and can use it. Further, one tends to use it in the best interest of oneself and one's neighbours, as one perceives it. If you believe this, you do not start with incentives, you start by observing and listening and then move to helping people analyze their own experience (if necessary), and helping them get additional information (if necessary).

The second assumption, which is too often ignored, is that community development starts where the people are and helps them go where they WANT to go. It is a process of personal and community growth, not simply one of target achievement (no matter how worthy the targets). Too often community development starts where an outside agency is and helps the people to go where the agency wants them to go — "for their own good," as the agency perceives it. Whose felt needs are being addressed? This does not imply that the needs perceived by the helping agency are not real, but it does imply that self-development is not likely to take place until those needs are clearly perceived by the people themselves and put at the top of their agenda.

Thus, the community development agency and its workers must keep their focus on the people and their development. It should truly be a process of education and growth toward a sense of competence and self-reliance. There will always be new problems and we can never solve them all, but we can help a community to develop an approach and a method for dealing with problems as they arise in a self-dependent manner. Thus, the community development worker must be an educator and enabler, even more than an 'organiser.'

Origins of UCD in India

Urban Community Development, in India had its origins in the government's rural community development programme. This commenced on October 2nd, 1952 and grew to cover more than five lakh villages in the Country. By the late 50's there was discussion and controversy about whether this approach could be used among the urban poor also.

Urban Community Development Today

As experience has been accumulating, certain changes have begun to take place in the more successful projects. Some of these are :

1. An emphasis upon economic activities such as small loans, production centres, vocational training.
2. More attention to housing for the poor.
3. Move towards linking urban community development with larger CITY (wide programmes of physical improvement such as environmental improvement and housing) : thus, integrating urban community development within a broader developmental process.
4. A move towards linking voluntary organizations with government and municipal organizations through urban community development.
5. A need to enhance the coordination and convergence of basic services for the urban poor and to assume that all are covered by these services.
6. More use is being made of community "volunteers," *i.e.* community level workers selected preferably from the community itself.
7. Finally, the present UCD projects do not begin with a pre-established set of services.

Concluding Caveat : Some Common Problems

1. One of the common problems arising out of the current UCD projects — particularly Hyderabad and Visakhapatnam

which have impressive and successful habitat programmes centering around self-help housing is that some cities wish to take up UCD projects as a means of solving their housing problems without going through the community development process.

2. The use of community volunteers is essential to the basic services strategy; however, there can be complicated consequences of this. For example, in Hyderabad, bustee sahayaks and community volunteers organized themselves into a union and demanded that they be put on a regular scale as municipal employees. This, in essence, defeats the purpose. Community volunteers are supposed to be genuine members of the community who serve as a link between the community and the formal service systems. Therefore, it is the view of this writer that they should work only part time in their roles as community volunteers so as to maintain their identification with the community.

3. We do not have sufficiently effective facilities for training field staff. A good CD worker is the key to the success of a project. If the field staff understand the CD approach and can work with people effectively, other problems can be dealt with. But this calls for non-traditional, field related, practical training which prepares trainees to deal with the problems and issues they meet daily and which reinforce their motivations, attitudes and skills.

4. We do not have good and enough monitoring and evaluation systems of a participatory nature. These are important for the field staff to correct errors as they go along.

5. Finally, there are not enough of us who really have faith and trust in the people and who understand that while we are "friends and philosophers," may be we should be ''gardeners" rather than guides/workers who help create the condition for people to grow and realize their own potential. In the old days of rural community development, we used to say we should "lead from behind". Today we should say with Gandhiji, "There go my people, I'm their leader, I must hurry and catch up with them."

16

Useful References in the Context of Urban Development

(A) UCD NEEDS TO BE IN A LOCAL BODY SETUP

Continuing arguments were there over the last three decades as to under which aegis these special programmes like UCD are to be administered in the urban areas. We have various examples where these programmes are directed and implemented by Urban Local Bodies, Urban Development Agencies, District Agencies, Slum Clearance Boards, N.G.Os., etc. with varying degrees of success, depending mostly on staff commitment, quality of local leadership and the human element. Municipal bodies are there not only to provide various physical amenities, and civic services, but also to maintain and upkeep them for continued utility by its citizens. In the case of development bodies, they get funds for specific projects and the assets created by them are treated for future maintenances and up-keep as the concern of the Urban Local Bodies. In all these cases, it looks as though a parallel administration is running in the urban limits, in which the local body has little or no concern.

Right type of manpower may not always be there, and the local bodies also tend to behave independent of the District Administration, by which they are deprived of many developmental services due to the citizens. They must be linked up with the District Chief and treated on par with other Development Officers. The 74th Amendment now has entrusted many new obligatory functions connected with various social and developmental responsibilities to the municipalities. As it is, even though some municipalities have no capacity to administer such tasks, they must be strengthened and enabled to do so in the near future. So on the plea that they are not capable of running a programme like UCD, this responsibility cannot be entrusted to some other agency. In the larger interest, it is always advisable to actively involve the urban local bodies and maintain the strong linkages, between them, their people and the district administration.

The urban local bodies should not only be the implementers of the UCD, but also have a stake in it and be made to own the programme as is the case with civil works, water supply etc., which are handled by them now. In the municipal budget, certain percentage of funds has to be reserved for the exclusive benefit of S.C., S.T., and Women and Child Development. All these allocations must form part of the budget of UCD and be implemented through NHCs. The staff recruited also must be treated as municipal staff directly subordinate to the Chief Executive just like any other municipal employee but not as a separate cadre. Convergence is an important principle in UBSP/UCD. The district chief must be made to ensure that all developmental services flow into different towns of the district.

There may be a district development Committee in which the municipalities indicate their needs related to health, education, industries, water, sanitation, Public distribution system, and various other welfare programmes and on a pro rata basis. These are to be ensured by the concerned District Officers with no disparity between rural and urban. By abiding to these guidelines, all the programmes benefiting the poor have to be necessarily implemented by local bodies concerned.

(B) THE SEVENTY-FOURTH CONSTITUTIONAL AMENDMENT

(A Facilitating Structure for Municipal Governments)

India's long history of urban municipal governance was characterized by some structural infirmities which affected its performance. Municipal bodies were designated limited powers. Their autonomy was restricted. The allocation of poor financial resources made them totally dependent on the state government.

Inadequacy in the services provided by municipalities raised doubts in the public mind about their ability to efficiently discharge their civic responsibilities. State governments were prone to taking the drastic step of superseding municipalities on grounds of malfunctioning and not following it up with elections at an early date. Political considerations often dominated the decisions.

The Seventy-fourth Constitution Amendment Act, 1992, brought about a radical departure from the past structure of local governance. Among other things, it :

- Makes the constitution of municipalities mandatory.
- Recognises a third tier of elected representatives below the Centre and States.
- Requires direct elections to a municipality (exceptions have been specified).
- Reserves one-third seats for women and also reserves seats for scheduled castes and tribes.
- Lays down a fixed tenure of five years for municipalities.
- Severely restricts the power of the State government to dissolve a municipality.
- Requires the State Finance Commission to review the financial position of Municipalities and make recommendations to the Governor in regard to taxation powers of the Municipality, revenue sharing and grants-in-aid.
- Requires the State Election Commission to conduct elections of municipalities and
- Makes the setting up of district planning committees, metropolitan committees and ward committees mandatory.

The Seventy-fourth constitutional amendment thus ensures the local urban governments are not at the mercy of the State Government. The stage has thus been set for municipal bodies to take up the challenge, draw up city plans of action and implement them through popular participation.

Twelfth Schedule (Article 243w)

1. Urban planning including town planning
2. Regulation of land use and construction of buildings

3. Planning for economic and social development
4. Roads and bridges
5. Water supply for domestic, industrial and commercial purposes.
6. Public health, sanitation conservancy and social waste management.
7. Fire services
8. Urban forestry, protection of the environment and promotion of ecological aspects.
9. Safeguarding the interests of weaker sections of society, including the handicapped and mentally retarded
10. Slum improvement and upgradation
11. Urban poverty alleviation
12. Provision of urban amenities and facilities such as parks, gardens, playgrounds.
13. Promotion of cultural, educational and aesthetic aspects.
14. Burials and burial grounds; crematoria, cremation grounds and electric crematoria.
15. Cattle pounds, prevention of cruelty to animals
16. Vital statistics including registration of births and deaths
17. Public amenities including street lighting, parking lots, bus stops and public conveniences.
18. Regulation of slaughter houses and tanneries.

(C) TYPES OF CHILDREN IN DIFFICULT CIRCUMSTANCES

Children constitute about 14% of the total population and if a family is undergoing hardships, the children are the first to suffer from them. For a poverty stricken illiterate TODAY is the immediate urgency and they do not believe "TODAY'S CHILD IS TOMORROW'S WORLD.'' So out of dire family conditions some of the children in poor families, not knowing what their rights are indulge in untoward and soon become victims of vice. They come under different categories which are explained below.

1. Child Labour

It has always been a phenomena in developing countries. They work in household industries, wayside eating places, repair shops and the manufacturing units. They also pick up scrap or waste for recycling and are also involved in vending of inexpensive goods.

Their early participation in work force causes :

Deprivation of their right to childhood,

To education,

To opportunities for development

To leisure and recreation

Affects their health

Nutritional status

Length of productive life

Psycho social development

The extent of damage to them depends upon

Nature and hours of work

Working conditions

Wages paid

Type of employer

Work environment

The age is usually between 5-14 years, but more so in 10-14 age group. Their number is varying anywhere between 5 to 10% but it is large enough to be a cause for national concern.

The child workers are usually present in informal sector as

- wage earners
- self-employed workers
- unpaid family workers
- apprentices
- bonded workers.

2. Street Children

1. Majority of them are over eight years

2. Most of them are boys (about 8% are girls)
3. Most of them have never attended school (2/3 illiterate)
4. Not all are recent migrants. Some have run away from homes. Some are drawn by city glamour.
5. Most children have ties with their families (77%)
6. Parents hold low paid unskilled jobs or are self-employed
7. Most street children work for a living
8. Majority of street children are self-employed
9. Their earnings and occupational mobility are limited.
10. Their nutrition and health status is unsatisfactory.
11. They are exposed to physical abuse and extortion.
12. The need to survive forces some of them to illegal activities
13. They have to struggle for daily survival and are forced to cope with the realities of adulthood and poverty at an young age.

The programme to protect street children and develop their capabilities include :

1. Economic — credit and training for skills development
2. Shelter — to those without homes, drop in centres for bath and toilet for others
3. Social services — NFE, health, supplemental nutrition
4. Welfare services — counselling and guidance to children and families, identity cards, recreation, liaise with police etc. to prevent them from harassment
5. Others — legal assistance, opportunities for socialisation, interaction.

3. Children in Need of Care and Protection (under JJ Act)

They include those deprived of a home care, neglected, destitute, victimised or delinquent. A child found begging without a home and without a means for sustenance is destitute. A child associating with a brother or a prostitute or other person leading immoral or drunken life or he is likely to be abused or exploited for immoral or illegal purposes — they also need care.

The programmes run by Government and NGOs for them include :

1. Children's homes or orphanages
2. SOS children's villages with 15 to 20 family homes each
3. Foster care for children of families facing a temporary crisis
4. Sponsorship programme by CCF; Terre Des Homes, Foster Parents, Plan International and Community Aid and Sponsorship Programme (CASP with sponsors from Canada, Australia, Netherlands and USA)
5. Adoption.

4. Children in Conflict with Laws

Those involved in vagrancy, crime and delinquency come under this category.

Delinquent is a young person (Boys of below 16 years and girls below 18 years of age) who violates law by committing a prohibited act — smoke, driving, sexually active, gambling, gang fights, extortion etc.

Most of them are between 12-16 years. 70% of juveniles apprehended are living with parents. 13% were homeless.

84% of offenders came from families with less than Rs. 1,000 income, 42% were illiterate, 32% are below primary level. Deviant behaviour cannot be solved by penal measures. Programmes mentioned for working, street and other categories of disadvantaged children would help in reducing deviance.

Children released need careful counselling. Communities must have early warning system to identify children who become marginalised from family, community, school etc. and start early intervention with the help of NGOs.

(D) HABITAT AND COMMUNITY DEVELOPMENT EXPERIENCE IN HYDERABAD

Hyderabd Urban Community Development Project

The rapid growth of urban areas in India has resulted in various urban problems which include housing and basic services to the poor and under privileged groups. Slums have emerged in the urban scene as the poor man's solution to the problem of housing. The traditional method of slum clearance was not found to be the proper answer and it was realised that any effort to solve slum problems must encourage participation of client groups.

The UCD Project in Hyderabad was quoted as a model for the successful implementation of developmental programmes for the urban poor and it is considered an ideal method of aiding the people to help themselves. The emphasis here is on prioritization of needs as defined by the people themselves and of efforts for self-help and self-reliance so as to make the development process more efficient, meaningful and durable. The UCD approach unlike the conventional physical developmental scheme, calls upon the community to evolve its own direction for the development, with the agency acting as a catalytic agent. It facilitates group thinking to deal with any problem and so provides relevant clues for future attempts in planning for slum improvement.

Self-help Housing-Habitat

At a time when housing is considered a non-remunerative venture attracting no loan assistance from banks or any other public agency, it was initiated as a self-help effort with the active involvement of people, service organisations and the Municipal Corporation of Hyderabad. The dwellers in 4 slums have got the title (through purchase) over the land they are residing and their felt need was money and more than that permission to construct a house from the local body, which is just impossible because of the prevailing building bylaws and rules in regard to minimum plot size and road width. Avoiding the attention of the planners concerned, UCD Project helped these highly motivated communities to go in for self-help housing, which has no comparison to the old shacked settlements they had earlier; but still in absolute violation of the building rules that were in vogue then. The higher-ups in politics and the officials in the bureaucracy were pleased with the outcome when these houses come up for inauguration and realised the need for relaxing the building bylaws. This was a welcome change for promotion of self-help housing activity in slums. More than this, the State Government formed a small official committee which was asked to enquire and come out with a list of unobjectionable slums where the land belongs to Government and other public bodies. Thus in October 1975, 13,500 title deeds for house sites were distributed to the actual dwellers in Hyderabad. It was also decided to link self-help housing as an additional activity of UCD project adding the engineering and planning wings to it, since it was better equipped to co-ordinate and integrate developmental efforts through involving people to change their own living environment.

The Habitat Programme, though conceptually distinct from UCD activities, added a new dimension to the project. The self-help housing in a significant way reduced construction costs and mobilized individual resources. It also enabled the beneficiary to cope up with the low quantum of institutional finance minimising the role of middlemen. A sense of pride, welcome change in attitude and an urge for better living with necessary change in prevailing life habits helped the poor to carve out a better future.

The strategy for finance was to link a particular slum to a nearby lending bank and to make loans available to the beneficiaries at differential rate of interest of 4 per cent per annum with provision for repayment in easy instalments and with loanees surrendering their pattas (land deeds) as security for the loans. The beneficiaries contribution was to the tune of 20 per cent of total cost of the unit estimated then at Rs. 6,200. Two thousand nine hundred seventy-three houses were constructed in 31 slums by about 1980 after which the Housing & Urban Development Corporation (HUDCO) came up in a big way.

HUDCO Loan

HUDCO first sanctioned loan to 7936 units at a total cost of over Rs. 69 million with the loan component limited to Rs. 48 million Project reports for additional 1739 units came in during 1987-88. Against an estimated cost of Rs. 12,000 on each unit, the loan component is Rs. 10,700 with an added subsidy of Rs. 1,000 from the State Government. The beneficiary contribution is limited to Rs. 300 which gave raise to a new indigenous mechanism, where local leader tend to play the role of contractor dominating the real poor. Studies recently made indicate that there has been a change in the entire programme implementation from a process orientation, where motivation and 'software' inputs were emphasised, to a target orientation one where provision of inputs was considered more important. This also marked a change in the level of participation by the communities at various stages with the housing introduced more as an induced need and not a really felt one. The financial system adopted earlier served to strengthen people's participation in development as a cost effective measure, but with HUDCO and government subsidy coming in, the project took to housing and environmental improvement as more of products where people's participation became negligible and process part not much emphasised.

(E) UCD PROJECT IN HYDERABAD ATTRACTED WORLD-WIDE ATTENTION

UCD project in Hyderabad attracted worldwide attention. UNICEF's Annual Report on the ''State of the World's Children" in 1989 has made a reference to the project. It says, "In Hyderabad the neighbourhoods, which are home to the poorest 25% of the city's families have been transformed, in the last ten years, into clean, well-knit settlements of modest brick houses with piped water and an efficient sewage system. With the participation of the community, the Urban Community Development Department brought a basic infrastructure of asphalt roads, electricity lines, tap water and underground drainages. Families were given the deeds to their own plot of lands, plus a 1000-rupee subsidy and a 7,000 rupee low-interest loan. With further 2000 rupees of their own capital, families could then construct their own home, normally consisting of two rooms and a separate toilet."

The report has, very correctly pointed out life has become happier and nearly equal to what middle classes would choose to live. But it is nonetheless a very significant improvement on what was in the past.

There could be no better description of the state of affairs in the slums of Hyderabad. What has happened has been characterized as something good. Good may not be good where better is expected. Yet, "it is a very significant improvement on what was". The slums of Hyderabad were as filthy and dirty as any ordinary slum. A vast majority of them are no longer filthy. There is no stagnant water, no rubbish around and no more hutments normally associated with a slum. You do not find children running around with running noses, playing in muddy pools of water or indulging in frequent fistfights. The slum children as also adults, look cleaner than they used to be a decade and a half ago.

(F) HYDERABAD URBAN COMMUNITY DEVELOPMENT PROJECT — EFFECT OF SHIFT IN EMPHASIS

Many studies have been undertaken to assess the impact of the large scale expansion of the Urban Community Development (UCD) Programme in the city of Hyderabad which has included the Habitat Programme. Some of the major findings of these studies are given below for the information of the implementing agencies and those involved in community development.

1. Community participation was considered to be the pivotal factor in determining the priority of developmental activities in UCD. But with the introduction of Habitat Programme, Housing became the essential component of its activities at the very entry point.
2. The financial system and management of UCD which was cost-effective, served to strengthen the people's participation. The system gave a fair opportunity to analyze the community's needs and problems with the ultimate objective of solving the problems with their own involvement. This provided a foundation for a strong organizational set-up which acted as a link between the people and the bureaucracy.

   However, as a result of financial assistance from Housing & Urban Development Corporation (HUDCO) and the governmental subsidy, housing and environmental improvement became delivery components overshadowing the people's participation.
3. When the Habitat Housing was initiated in 1975, there was a genuine question raised "How can UCD build 13,000 houses?" There came the quick response — "UCD is not constructing 13,000 houses; but there are 13,000 families who construct their own houses and

UCD is only a catalyst in promoting this goal." "But from the subsequent policies, practices and funding procedures, there arose a doubt whether there are some community leaders in slums at middle level, who act as contractors defeating the basic principle of community involvement and beneficiary participation.

4. The poorest of the poor in the slum communities had to be identified as a separate target group for assistance. This was not really the case and thus there were cases where some houses were left incomplete, and the inmates were compelled, to dispose of their plots and once again join the homeless.
5. Too many middle level interventions made the housing programme more bureaucratic affecting the interaction between the UCD staff and the beneficiaries. There were also the so-called slum leaders and representatives who very often interpreted things to their own advantage.
6. Rules facilitating the conditional title deeds provided to the beneficiaries were laudable. However, laxity in strictly enforcing them (because of political interference) led to (a) fictitious sales at throw away prices and (b) repayment defaults on loan instalments.
7. Adequate information and guidance on the housing plan was not given to the beneficiaries which resulted in improper utilization of resources. This further led to financial crises and in turn weakened the prospects of house completion.
8. Environmental improvement was not systematic and not taken up at the right time. It was launched with the involvement of contractors. As such, the commitment of the slum dwellers to maintain and benefit from the amenities provided initially, was not forthcoming.
9. Same was the case with regard to software inputs to improve the standard of living. The poor did not fully exploit the benefits from various services.
10. As the volume of work and operation increased, the administrative set up also grew in size. This adversely

affected the quality of work and commitment of workers. The initial successes which witnessed remarkable participation from the beneficiaries (where the UCD presented itself as an informal and friendly organisation) was no more evident as the organisation expanded. UCD became another bureaucratic institution.

11. The flexibility in recruiting staff, the privilege which was enjoyed earlier, thinned out and the recruitment of field staff was taken up on a large scale. UCD started to select candidates from the employment exchanges thus reducing the scope for picking up local enthusiastic people who form the real backbone of the community development processes. The involvement and enthusiasm of this newly recruited staff was of a lesser degree since they could not maintain the social and ethnic ties with the local communities as effectively as the local leaders. They started seeing their role as mere overseers and protectors of rules.

12. The very basic objective of the UCD Project is to motivate the communities to identify their priorities, and their needs and find ways and means to fulfil them. But the introduction of the HUDCO housing scheme brought a conceptual change in the UCD Project. In the operational system that followed, the local leaders who were hitherto considered as catalysts, were compelled to remain as mere abiders of the scheme showing little concern for the felt needs of the communities. Of course, in few cases where the leadership is of democratic nature, the interests of the community members were protected.

13. Activities other than physical and tangible inputs, were given less priority as they are felt to be time consuming with results not quite perceptible in the absence of active community involvement.

14. In spite of all the developmental efforts, the usual phenomenon is that the slums increase in number year after year. Services are free and taxes are none and no one would like to lose this privilege. There should be strong political will to initiate suitable measures to remove

the slums from that category soon after the necessary infrastructure is created.

15. India is a huge country with 25 States and Union Territories and there is bound to be misconception even today on this self-help housing programme. It should be understood in the right perspective.

17

UCD in Vijayawada and Visakhapatnam

UCD in Hyderabad has been successful not only in implementing socio-economic programmes but also in promoting and carrying out self-help housing programme on a large scale. Seeing these results, the authorities of Visakhapatnam Urban Development Authority wanted to replicate Urban Community Development in Visakhapatnam Municipal Corporation making Self-help housing as the entry point with UNICEF assistance. One Project Officer, Sri D.G. Rama Rao and a Deputy Project Officer, Smt. B. Venkatreswari were deputed to Visakhapatnam from Hyderabad for initiating and directing the project. With a Director and 2 Project Officers assisted by 11 Community organisers this project has carried out both housing and community development activities on the same lines as in Hyderabad but with minor differences in emphasis to suit the local conditions.

Vijayawada came into operation in 1983 in a few slums. But with UNICEF assistance it grew into a massive programme with positive impact from 1986 onwards. Women's groups have been organised systematically in all slums and with the cooperation and assistance of Shramik Vidya Peeth, Vijayawada, a number of income generation activities for women were taken up yielding satisfactory results. Some of the accomplishments in this regard are given below.

Coffee Powder Business

Mrs. D.V. Subbalakshmi and her friends also found a ready market in Ajit Singh Nagar for the ground coffee powder. There was opposition from her husband when she expressed a desire to supplement the family income. It was against the family traditions for women to work. But Mrs. Subbalakshmi had her way. She and others were trained by Shramik Vidyapeeth to manufacture coffee powder and pack them in polythene bags. Her efforts have not been in vain. She draws an income of Rs. 800 per month as her share of the profits from the business. Coffee seeds are purchased from the Coffee Board. The Shramik Vidyapeeth has provided the grinder.

Sodas to Quench Thirst

Mrs. Manikyamma, Mrs. T. Narasamma and Miss M. Anita were provided with the necessary units to fill soda bottles. The UCD provided two-thirds of the amount necessary while the Shramik Vidyapeeth gave the balance. The understanding is that the beneficiaries should repay 50% of the total amount after two years. If they did so, the entire unit would become their own.

The women of the household were content with doing the domestic chores. The Neighbourhood Committees have sponsored the scheme. Mrs. Manikyamma underwent training in bottling soda water. The Shramik Vidyapeeth trained her and made available the unit to the group. Her husband, who sold betel leaves and cigarettes in a small kiosk, was selling the bottles. The soda-bottling unit was augmenting the family income by Rs. 600 per month. The women are normally content with doing domestic chores. This is a welcome change.

Detergent Soap

Sarojini Devi Vanita Mandali is one of the fifteen NHCs in Ajit Singh Nagar. Mrs. K. Ammulu, Mrs. V. Parvathi, Mrs. B. Mahalaxmi and Miss Shiakh Madina are helping to keep the clothes of the people clean. They manufacture detergent cakes and surf powder. UNICEF provided nearly 66 per cent of the cost of the machinery and the Shramik Vidyapeeth made good the balance. A nationalized bank provided the working capital of Rs. 14,000. Once the bank loan is repaid and half the cost of the Unit refunded, the entire machinery will become theirs. They have already cleared half the bank loan. They would become owners, undoubtedly, as working on only two days in a week; they are making a clear profit of Rs. 1,000 per month.

Rolled Gold Ornaments

Like flowers and kumkum, ornaments are an attraction for women. They must wear at least glass bangles. Those who can afford it go in for gold ornaments. The less fortunate go in for rolled-gold bangles, necklaces, ear rings and nose studs. Made of copper, the ornaments are gold plated. Machilipatnam, the District Headquarters for Krishna District, in which Vijayawada is located, is famous for its gold plating industry. All that glitters may not be gold. The women would, however, like to wear glittering ornaments.

Allu Anuradha and four others have formed a group to make ornaments from copper and baser material. They sell it to manufacturers in Machilipatnam for gold plating them. The group gets Rs. 1,500 per month.

They feel they would be able to garner much more if they could also gold plate the ornaments. Anuradha said "that is our next aim."

Chaitanya Mahila Neighbourhood Committee

The women, who for centuries had been in deep slumber, have begun to wake up. They are realising their potential. The days when they shed silent tears over their fate are gone. This is especially true of the women of Vidyadharapuram, a notified slum area in Vijayawada. They have given a clarion call to other women folk to join them in their march forward, towards emancipation and eventual progress. Having been denied facilities all these years; they have suddenly become aware of their place in society. Like a hungry man trying to consume as much as possible, they are endeavouring to learn as much as possible. They are eager to have all that they missed out over the years.

The credit for utilizing the Urban Community Development programmes to the maximum extent possible — rather, a little more than that too — must go to the Chaitanya Mahila Neighbourhood Committee in this area. It has achieved something which no other NHC, either under UBS or UCD, has achieved.

(a) *Dance Class*

Vidhyadharapuram is the first slum to have cultural classes. The honorarium for the dance teacher is met from the UCD funds.

The authorities would not agree to this expenditure being debited to the UCD accounts. But the NHC would not give up. "We have already conducted the classes for two months. We have committed ourselves to teach the children dancing. If we now discontinue the classes, we would be disappointing the young ones." The committee made one plea after another until the authorities relented.

(b) *Music Class*

Music classes are also being conducted. Twenty students are being taught Karnatic music. Raising contributions from the parents of the children concerned, however, is paying the remuneration for the teacher. Thus there is public contribution for this effort.

(c) *Mass Literacy*

Vidyadharapuram is also leading in the matter of holding classes under the Mass Literacy Programme. Ten literate members of the area hold classes individually. Ten to twenty persons attend these classes. These organisers, as they are called, made 200 persons literate last year. The second batch is now learning to read and write.

Mrs. K. Seshamani, one such organiser and the Secretary of the NHC, said that as the students were mostly adults they were able to learn fast. By attending the classes regularly for 1½ to 2 hours each day, they were able to reach the standard prevailing in class III in three months. Those who completed the course were now able to write letters. They transacted business with the banks, they are able to fill up necessary forms for securing loans etc.

What do the organisers, the teachers, who hold these classes get? Mrs. Seshamani replied "the supreme satisfaction of having made somebody literate." She pointed out that the sacred Indian Scriptures had specifically mentioned that 'Vidyadaanam' was the best 'daanam' one could give. By teaching others, there was no diminishing the skills of the teacher. What was given to the learner, could not be taken away by another person. Still UNICEF has provided some money to provide gifts to such volunteers.

(d) *Manava Seva is Madhava Seva*

What made her take up this work, though it was not remunerative, as the teachers did not get even a token honorarium? Mrs.

TAILORING CENTRE

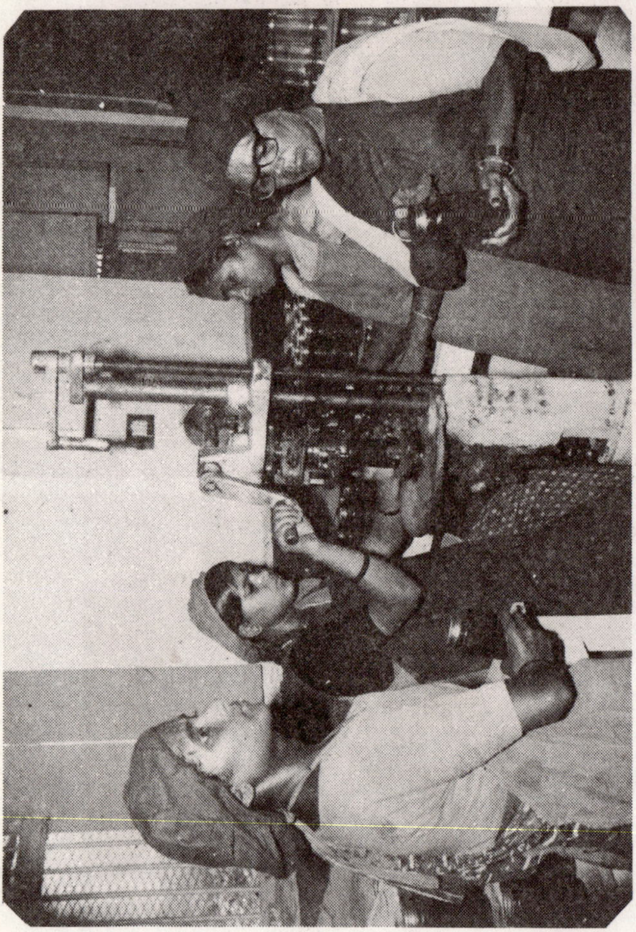

PICKLES UNIT UNDER HYDERABAD UCD

Seshamani said she was encouraged by her father, before her marriage, to undertake social work as "Manava Seva is Madhava Seva" — "Service to fellowmen is service to God." "Fortunately for me, my husband also encourages me."

(e) *Balwadis and Sewing Class*

Vidyadharapuram is situated on the slopes of the hill, which is the abode of the presiding deity of Vijayawada — Goddess Kanaka Durga. It is here that the sewing classes, the balwadi and the cultural classes are held in the temporary community hall. The women are determined to stand on their own feet and not be a burden to the family economically.

(f) *Creche or Balwadi*

There are 200 households under the NHC. 150 of them have individual two-pit low cost sanitation latrines. Thirty infants are being looked after in a creche. They are mostly the children of vegetable vendors who go to the wholesale market early in the morning and make retail sales of the vegetables they buy. The mothers are able to go out and transact business and earn, because their children are looked after in the creche or balwadi.

18

Hyderabad UCD in Development of Women and Children

Convergence of services is one of the most important factors in accelerating an improvement in the quality of life of women and children with respect to home, health, education, economic status and awareness. For example :

1. For improving the home situation :
   - Providing safe drinking water, better drainage and sewer systems.
   - Helping families to build houses rather than shanties.
   - Providing latrines, both community and private.
2. For improving the health status of women and children :
   - Systematic immunizations and medical check-up.
   - Supplementary nutrition for children between 0-5 years both in and outside of nursery schools.
3. For improving the literacy rate of women and children :
   - Adult literacy Centres.
   - Coaching classes for students and dropouts.
   - Pre-primary schools which enhance school readiness for children whose parents never attended school.
4. For improving the economic status of women :
   - Training in skills which save costs (*e.g.* sewing, sewing machine repairs) or help earn extra income (*e.g.* making pickles, spices)
   - Group income-generating activities.

- Arranging for low interest bank loans for self-employed women *e.g.* street vendors of vegetables, fruits etc.

5. For increasing awareness and widening the horizons of women :

   - Information as to who can be contacted for what assistance *e.g.* family planning measures, civic amenities.
   - Organizing study tours to places of pilgrimage educational and historical interest, within the city the state and to other states.
   - Arranging get-togethers on various important national days and festivals.
   - Educational film shows.
   - Making available community radio and TV sets.

19

Rural Community Development Experience

Except for couple of years, I was totally involved in Extension and Community Development line, the initial period of 10 years being in Rural Community Development as Extension Officer and Block Development Officer and thereafter in Urban Community Development for over 13 years as Project Officer and Director. I served for another 10 years as Project Officer in UNICEF in the same field. With my experience in all these fields, my feeling is that the philosophy of human approach and community participation are nearly the same in both rural and urban areas. Both communities have sentimental and psychological similarities but with slight difference in degree. The cohesiveness of the communities is also in variance in rural and urban areas. I wish to place on record some of the notable experiences.

As Extension Officer in 1950's

As Extension Officer, I was posted to a very backward Panchayat Samithi where it was decided to introduce pedigree bulls to upgrade quality of local cows and buffalos. Earlier, the officers of Animal Husbandry department used to buy the animals on their own and supply the pedigree bulls at half cost for which there used to be a lot of criticism. The situation motivated me to take one or two representatives from the villages to the cattle shandy to select Ongole bulls of their choice and bargain the price also. I did so. At first they saw different animals and felt either the quality is not up to the mark or the cost is more. But they had to buy one as they could not return empty handed. So with the second round of visits on subsequent days they chose animals and bargained the price. Thus they were satisfied and involved which is most important from the community development angle.

About 8 bulls were purchased, a lorry was hired and they were loaded into it. Some sat in the lorry cabin by turns and the rest watched the animals in the open body. On the way one of the base wooden planks gave way and the leg of one bull went down that hole. It was hell for the village leaders. One of them went underneath the lorry body, put his head below the leg and slowly pushed it to the top and saved the animal from getting its leg fractured.

After going home, they were very happy with their experiences and with a grand procession, the animals with leaders were welcomed into the respective villages. This is what we should mean by community involvement.

Another interesting and funny experience was the purchase of Murrah pedigree buffalos, which are hefty in size compared to the local animals. Six villages have agreed to go in for these animals after prolonged motivation during night times which was their leisure time. The representatives were taken to the Government farm at Visakhapatnam. The travel and stay in hotel was of course an exciting experience which they could not forget. They went to the Dairy farm and saw the animals. The head of the Murrah buffalo was very big and they felt that their she-buffalos will die if big calves are born after they are mated with these bulls. Then the example of bulky and heavy husband and his puny wife with their children had to be given. This convinced them to some extent and they finally opted for young buffalo bulls, even though they take some time to get matured for service. This is because they are smaller in size now and they felt the villagers will be slowly acquainted as the animals get bigger in size with age.

Another Anguish

There was one Mr. Kancharla Chandrayya in the group who chose one bull for his village. After entering the village he was nicknamed as dunnapothu (buffalo) Chandrayya. It took time for the animal to serve the buffalos even though it became big. Then he was called goddumothu (impotent) Chandrayya. Finally after it started playing its legitimate role, his name was reverted back to Kancharla Chandrayya.

Cattle Show

There is a remote town adjacent to the reserve forest and people there are cattle lovers. One will be surprised to note that one farmer used to feed his pet bulls with cooked rice as part of feed which is symbolic of his love. There are very strong factions in the town which do not see eye to eye. But the author as Extension officer was good to every one and the idea of organising a cattle show was mooted. A committee for raising funds was formed involving rival groups and it was the first time for people to see the rival leaders travelling in the same bullock cart with the Extension officer in between. Huge amounts had been collected and three ministers were invited. At that time the District officer commented that one dozen cattle shows can be conducted with the same amount.

You Enjoy Learning and Getting Benefited from People

We used to contact farmers in those days for Small Savings. One elderly person asked me about my family, children and the cost of cigarettes that I smoke per day/month/year. Then he exclaimed — Grandson! how can you come and ask me for small savings and thrift when you yourself are not practicing it. I gave up that habit on the very day and so I am able to reach my 70th year in age, let alone the savings, I made.

As a Block Development Officer (BDO)

Rural Community Development is a failure as some people say. But out of my experience over the last 4 decades, I would argue it is not so. Its philosophy is excellent for all times; but its practice only went astray for which the accountability is on the Implementers, Politicians and Planners. Planners too because — at one time they have categorized different districts and areas into backward and very backward and said no contribution is necessary from the beneficiaries in such areas. This is a wrong step on their part as there is no community development without community participation and we cannot ignore the potential of the vast human resource. This led to so many malpractices.

I still remember when I went as BDO to a backward area in early 60's, I found to my surprise that there was so much clamour for additional drinking water wells. The number of wells sanctioned for a panchayat depends upon the power and influence wielded by the local sarpanch and not on the actual need or norms. The more the number of wells sanctioned, the more commission the sarpanch or his henchmen get as there was no need for bidding and full payment is possible according to estimate. This is what I mean by political spoils and as a true community worker, I did not allow it to continue. With the executive powers vested in the BDO, I resorted to inviting bids and was able to get the work done at 20 to 30% less. Then the tempers rose high and the issue was moved in Zilla Parishad meeting. Do you know what I said to them? "As a BDO I am the custodian of public money and am supposed to use it in a prudent and intelligent way. I am also supposed to respect the decisions of the democratic body and act on their behalf to get work done. In this particular situation, I feel to my conscience, I am doing both. Please tell me how I am wrong." This silenced everybody and afterwards I got a pat from the District Collector, of course.

When I went to another Panchayat Samithi, I found the fertilizers were going into black market then. When the situation was analysed, I found the stocks were being purposely lifted at odd times, when agricultural operations are not there and so the distinguished few made a buck out of it. I brought this to the notice of the District Collector and requested him to postpone the releases till the next cropping season. So the cooperatives have to return empty handed without stocks and that gave rise to anger in some and it was placed before the general body meeting and the BDO was criticised for depriving the area with its legitimate quota. But when the facts were explained, everybody felt happy except the few with vested interests. The area was not deprived. It got extra quota in the next season.

As Panchayat Samithi Chief, one has got ample opportunities to innovate new practices. In 1960's, Primary Education was totally under the management of Panchayat Samithis. As Block Development Officer my observation was "Some primary schools were very good with efficient and sincere teachers. Some were really bad, with low syllabus coverage leaving the pupils as ultimate sufferers." In an effort to rectify the situation, a meeting of all Head Masters was called and our Deputy Inspector of Schools suggested that we must follow a realistic syllabus and every school must complete that without fail. To assess the performance of each school, we had convinced the teachers to agree for a common examination for 3rd to 5th standards. To encourage meritorious schools and students, some momentos were also instituted.

Thus there was healthy rivalry created. The Deputy Inspector of Schools, Mr. Appa Rao had set the question papers and got them printed confidentially. They were sent to schools in sealed covers. This had yielded good results in improving the teaching performance and aiming at coverage of total syllabus. But this did not continue for long.

Some Extension Officers felt it as an unnecessary burden and tried for transfers on grounds of ill-health etc. and the superior officers also started obliging them. When the whole matter was explained to the District Collector, he immediately sent a D.O. letter to district heads instructing them not to transfer any body from my Panchayat Samithi without his knowledge. That was the type of co-operation and support that we, as BDOs used to get from District Collectors.

Family Planning Advocacy

I was married in 1951 and after getting two daughters, the idea of limiting my family came into mind. This was gauged by my mother, who insisted strongly that I must have a son before I think of anything. This made me reconcile myself, which resulted in a third daughter. I felt it was high time then and so I went to a Private Nursing Home and got vasectomy performed in 1957 with an expenditure of over Rs. 300 in those days, when family planning department was unheard of.

I went as BDO (Block Development Officer) in 1959 and during the field visits I came across several farmers who said in different versions that their grandfathers were very well of, but the financial status was reduced now because of the large family size in the earlier two generations, which reduced the land holding from 40 acres to 8 acres with 5 sons, and 8 acres to 2 acres to the present generation.

"How many sons do you have now and what is it that you can give to your children? Is the question posed."

Many are of confirmed opinion that vasectomy operation is an absolute need; but they had their own doubts regarding male potency and ability to do hard work after operation. For this I gave my own example and it worked.

Ninety three farmers agreed to undergo family planning operation. Since there was no family planning department in 1961, we had to request the District Medical Officer to depute some doctors to our Primary Health Centre and get the camp organised. Through this the farmers believed that a great help was given to them. The vasectomy camps became a regular feature after this, which used to attract large number of beneficiaries even without incentives.

This is what a need based programme means wherein you provide sufficient information and motivate them leaving the ultimate decision to their wisdom and choice.

My Samithi Headquarters was not jeepable and one has to wallow across a small river to reach that place. It was rainy season and the District Collector sent his tour programme for my office inspection. I went to the other side of the river to receive him. But I got a jolt, when he said, I am supposed to come on my own and you need not have come here. Such were the righteousness of many officers in those days.

In another Panchayat Samithi, I took the District Collector to an interior village for inspection. There was sudden down pour of rain on our way back and the jeep stuck in the muddy ditches. We had to walk for over 2 miles to reach a nearby village. Such instances also did not hurt the senior officers. I still remember one District Officer used to have a sigh of relief after he came out of our Samithi and said, "At last, we have entered the civilized world."

After completing my M.S. in U.S.A., I approached my Secretary in Panchayat Raj department for a posting. That was the precise time when a senior Special Grade BDO from a Panchayat Samithi was suspended on graft charges and the two rival parties were trying their best to have their choice candidate for that post. My Secretary advised me to join there immediately. The political rivalry there is such that the two parties have equal number of members in Panchayat Samithi and so they have to choose a neutral person as President, who happened to be an Ex-M.L.A. (Member of Legislative Assembly) and a stalwart in politics. I was just in my mid-thirties in age then and he considered me as a kid before my predecessor, who was suspended earlier. Without losing time, the President sent a note asking me to transfer some teachers. I returned the note back saying "I want to understand the position first before doing that." And that silenced him. Such incidents occurred many a times. When I was relieved on transfer, he was the first man to congratulate me and said "your predecessor went out with rebukes; but you, though young have proved yourself to be very friendly to every one; but at the same time behaved like a lion before the real guilty."

If circumstances warranted we used to be very dashing in those days. I was a Special grade BDO at a place where 2 big rivers join together. One river suddenly came into floods (no real flood warnings in those days) and my supervisory officer with his headquarters at the banks of the other river did not know this. Immediately I took a launch and proceeded against the stream to rescue all the persons, who were clinging on trees and roof tops. Rice was also taken from the local ration shops and food was supplied to all victims. The immediate supervisor (a senior person) called for an explanation for doing all this without orders; but my District Collector complimented me for this bold and timely initiative.

Policy, Executive and Judiciary were the important pillars of our Constitution of India and they were all mutually supplementary and complementary without encroaching on each other. If any violation occurs, they used to be immediately thwarted. One senior Minister in State Government in a public meeting used some harsh words against his Secretary, who visited the same place few days later and said "I can resign my post and become a Politician (minister) tomorrow. The other side cannot cherish this." Another Officer of mine in Community Development once wrote to all of us. "You have to act with love and compassion towards every one; but at the same time you cannot allow your weapon of punishment to be rusted." These sayings always ring in my mind.

So I say the Community Worker must be bold, frank and outright and need not get frightened by anybody. His strength is the community backup. This was the situation and experience of about four decades past.

Recently our organisation (UPACOR) handled community based Hand Pump Maintenance programme with UNICEF assistance in some villages and we wish the hand pump users should own it and not treat it as a government property and thus not answerable for anything that happened to it. For this we are trying to motivate the local communities to improve the environs around the hand pump and ensure the water that they get from it is potable. The response is not uniformly encouraging and I am often reminded that times have changed.

Is it true?

Is it the right trend?

Who is responsible?

Can we afford to ignore the vast inexhaustive human resource, people's involvement and community participation which brings life and pride to any activity?

The answer must come from today's politicians and bureaucrats. They must all realise the huge sums they spend from government has very little value compared to the humble inputs that are realised from the local beneficiaries. They bring in the pride and satisfaction that the programme is 'ours'. There is too much dependence created amongst the masses by doling funds and keeping people as mere spectators, which is a very dangerous trend. By this we are only damaging the human fabric for the sake of cheap popularity or votes and pushing the country to grave risk and utter degradation. Charity has no meaning in community work and the joy and beauty lies in group action with needy and just external support. The community worker should always go by these truths.

Community Worker must be above Parties and Politics

In one panchayat samithi soon after elections, one aged person was elected as president. He was a fatherly figure and he was asked whether he would still work on party basis or he would cooperate with everyone irrespective of party affiliation and politics. He said "I am elected by my group no doubt; but now I represent the entire population. So my acts and deeds would also be unbiased." With this right approach, he commanded respect from each and every body and his decisions were also very fair. This should be emulated by every political worker.

20

Institutional Arrangement and Capacity Building for Service Provision for Urban Poor in Hyderabad

(Scenario after introducing SIP Programme)

Staffing Pattern of U.C.D.

U.C.D. was started in Hyderabad on a pilot project basis during December, 1967 in Old City of Hyderabad (Ward-22). The Community Organisers worked in pairs and covered approximately 10,000 population per pair. Then the staff of UCD included one Project Officer and 8 Community Organisers only. By 1976 UCD covered 3 more project areas covering 52 slums and 60,000 population. The expenditure was Rs. 1.3 lakhs per project area. During 1979 with an additional 9 projects sanctioned by government, 2 additional posts of Project Officers, 3 Deputy Project Officers, and 9 Social Workers were sanctioned.

The launching of Urban Community Development (UCD) and Slum Improvement Programme in Hyderabad (HSIP) can be broadly put under the following phases :

UCD initiated by Government of India as a National plan activity with State Government, Local body and Community participation from 1967 till 1970 (4th Plan).

UCD initiated by State Government (under State sector) with Local body and community participation till 1977.

UCD with involvement of UNICEF and Banks for Self-help housing till around 1980.

DISTRIBUTION OF SAPLINGS

UCD with State Government, UNICEF, HUDCO and community participation till 1984.

Hyderabad Slum Improvement Project (HSIP) with Government, Overseas Development Administration (ODA), HUDCO and Municipal Corporation (MCH) participation in Phases I to III.

HSIP-I was only done haphazardly in few selected slums by providing Environmental Improvement and Shelter Upgradation. But the targets could not be reached. Hence in Phase II, plans (both physical and financial) were made well in advance and monitoring systems were inbuilt. Even baseline surveys were conducted.

By 1984 under HSIP-II programme in 210 slums covering 72,830 families was taken up with an expenditure of Rs. 155.7 millions. In April 1987 under HSIP-III another 300 slums (76,000 families) were taken up for development at a cost of Rs. 335.4 millions. At that time the staff of UCD was as follows (for 12 projects) :

Director	1	Dy. Engineer	1
Project Officer	6	Asst. Engineer	12
Dy. Project Officer	9	Asst. Town planner	1
Com. Organisers	24	Town Planning Assts.	4
Basti Sahayak	85	Draftsmen	12
Social Worker	9		

During 1996-97 after HSIP has withdrawn its support, the staffing pattern of UCD is as follows :

Director	1	Dy. Exe. Engineer	1
Project Officers	6	Asst. Engineers	12
Dy. Project Officers	9	Asst. Town Planner	1
Com. Organisers	6	Draftsmen	12
Com. Dev. Officers	18	Supdt.	1
Slum Dev. Officers	64	UDC/LDCs	16
Social Workers	9	Attenders	12

Medical Officer	1	Town Planning Assts.	4
		Chowkidar	1

UCD functions with the State Government and Municipal Corporation of Hyderabad (MCH) financial assistance. During 1996-97 Government gave Rs. 30 lakhs and MCH gave Rs. 75.98 lakhs, out of which nearly Rs. 82 lakhs was spent on pay and allowances of the staff thus leaving only Rs. 18 lakhs for UCD activities.

General Activities and Finance

1. Special Nutrition Programme : Wholly a Govt. of Andhra Pradesh Programme, which released Rs. 3 lakhs per annum.
2. Balwadis, Sewing centres etc. utilising local women / unemployed girls, as Neighbourhood Committee teachers / instructors in Youth organisations, Mahila mandals by providing 70 per cent of total expenditure as subsidy.
3. Intensive tree plantations for clean and green environment. 9000 tree guards were supplied in slums.
4. E.W.S. Housing : This is transferred from MCH to District Manager (Housing) under the administrative control of District Collector, Hyderabad. MCH has constructed 21,000 individual self-help EWS Housing units in different slums, with HUDCO's assistance.
5. Nehru Rozgar Yojana : Now merged in SJSRY.
6. Voluntary Garbage Removal Programme (VGRP) in slums / localities was launched in 1995-96 to promote communities to volunteer for better sanitation. UCD officials motivated slum people to start this programme and a tricycle rickshaw worth Rs. 4,000 as one time grant, is supplied by MCH to local organisations. Nodal agency collects Rs. 5 to Rs. 10 from each house and this programme is in operation in 167 slums.
7. Conducting programmes like Prajala Vaddaku Palana, Janma Bhoomi, IPP in slums through peoples participation.
8. Entrusting utility and maintenance of community halls to local community based organisations.

Capabilities of Various Departments Working for Urban Poor

1. UCD with its present staff of 40 Government cadre staff and 70 MCH cadre staff and 64 S.D.Os has to look after 811 slums covering 12.6 lakh population. At present in each circle, project officer's posts are vacant and they are managed by C.D.Os/C.Os. Sizable number of S.D.Os are working as bill collectors and administration assistants. Thus the man-power allocation and utilisation is not done properly, while the task remains the same if not mounting, day by day.

   To get quality work in UCD, the staff should be properly trained to have a mind set for 'community approach' — not the office room approach and they should be given regular, refresher field training by experienced consultants. The course material should be prepared / changed periodically based on the demands of the urban poor — by conducting need assessment surveys periodically in sample slums so that the content of the curriculum will be the context relevant and serves the purpose.

2. The engineering department has also qualified staff but their number seem to be rather inadequate.

Cost of various Infrastructure Activities under HSIP-II in Hyderabad Slums

S. No.	Agencies	Cost (lakh Rs.)
1.	Civil Infrastructure provided by MCH including LCS	1207.57
2.	APSEB	112.33
3.	Hyderabad Metro Water Works	170.48
4.	Health and Social Inputs	31.84
5.	Documentation Cell	14.79
6.	Evaluation	20.00
	TOTAL	1,557.01

Under HSIP-III

Programme-wise Overall Project Cost and Physical Targets

S. No.	Items	Quantity	Cost (lakhs)
1.	WBM/BT Roads (sq. mts.)	372558	313.953
2.	Sewerlines (Rmt.)	71055	88.818
3.	SW Drains (Rmt.)	20699	89.397
4.	SS Flooring (sq. mts.)	93214	54.332
5.	Insp. Chamber (No.)	27950	139.751
6.	Comm. Lat. (Seats)	241	19.430
7.	Comm. Halls (No.)	6107	88.105
8.	Septic Tanks (No.)	27	13.350
9.	L.C. Sanitation (No.)	12000	48.000
10.	Street Lights (No.)	2170	76.745
11.	Transformer (No.)	68	68.000
12(a)	Public Stand Post (No.)	527	
12(b)	Private Pipe Conn.	8396	135.980
	TOTAL		1135.860

Pricing of H.R.D. Programmes

	Rs. (lakhs)
(i) Health programme	75.54
(ii) Literacy and Education :	
(a) Adult literacy	14.94
(b) pre School Education	57.20
(iii) Economic Support Programme (13500 members)	53.50

Recovery Position

During 1996-97 ten housing schemes were attempted by UCD through A.P.U.D. and H.C. The recovery of loans to HUDCO was to the tune Rs. 363.52 lakhs collected from the beneficiaries.

From 1997-98 layout plans of 12 slums for housing programme were prepared and furnished to District Collector, Hyderabad.

Repayment of loan to HUDCO is Rs. 48.5 lakhs (Rs. 412.10 lakhs cumulative amount) which included Rs. 33.58 lakhs remitted by A.P.S.H.C. Ltd. to HUDCO as loan on behalf of MCH.

In the earlier stages the percentage of loans repaid was far from satisfactory. Though estimates may vary the figure was not beyond 50 per cent.

The reasons are many :

- poorly available resources of slum dwellers
- previous debts take precedence
- motivation is lacking for repayment
- No systematic programme for recovery — because of a confusion as to whether or not it is the responsibility of UCD or Revenue Department.
- Defaulting also seems to be encouraged by some political and slum leaders who treat this as a subsidy to the poor.

In 1992 the number of slums were 662. However due to pressures, the number of slums has risen to 811 during 1994 through renotification of some old slums. This shows the political manoeuvrability and vote bank nature of importance to slums. Unless one pays the entire amount, the patta papers which were under pledge with MCH / HUDCO would not be released. Then only the ownership could be claimed by the dwellers. As the land costs had escalated in the recent past drastically raising the asset value, most of the dwellers have been repaying the loan amount towards housing. Most of those who have taken Rs. 7,000 during first batch repaid completely. Many of those who have taken in the second batch of Rs. 13,000 have repaid to a large extent. However in case of self-employment schemes, the records relating to the recovery of loans are with the respective agencies (Banks, financial corporations etc.). As UCD acts only as a facilitator, no records are maintained with UCD.

21

Lessons Learnt from the Past S.I.P. in Hyderabad

HSIP has mainly focussed on environmental improvement with little stress on community participation. Thus it has just brought in quantitative change in living conditions of the few selected slums. Amenities alone could not improve the environment unless their maintenance is assured.

The target approach in Phase III HSIP changed the image of the UCD programme and the gap between people and project was widened as the element of consulting and involving people was totally neglected.

Staff recruitment and training received least priority unlike in other wings of the same HSIP programme. In the earlier UCD, the staff though limited was able to meet the challenges and applied UCD philosophy in right spirit with encouraging results.

With the ever increasing urban population, the ability of the City administration became much worse to tackle the problems of urban poor. UCD approach alone could be an effective and low cost option.

The underemphasis of community participatory process and self-help approach in the recent years in HSIP as an outcome of external assistance had proved to be a costly mistake warranting immediate correction. If not the repercussions would have been very severe for this faulty approach.

There was need for more community managed programmes and the bureaucracy must have willingly relinquished power to local people to administer and manage certain Basic Services programmes. The greatness of bureaucracy lies more in devolving and delegating more and more of its responsibilities to the local groups with suitable supportive incentives and assistance.

UCD is a multi-disciplinary and integrated programme, unique to Hyderabad, which slowly spread all over in the country.

With the launching of SIP programmes in Hyderabad, UCD activities and its philosophy had been toned down and human development focus pushed to low priority. Physical developmental plans were not discussed with communities and people's involvement was not much evident.

In HSIP phase III there was overemphasis on physical improvement at the cost of socio-economic inputs. The budget proposed under socio-economic programme for one year was sufficed for the total plan period, which reflects on the importance given to UCD.

UCD staff instead of moving in slums expected the slum communities to approach them in office.

So far 3 S.I.Ps were implemented in Hyderabad, with onus on UCD as the main / sole actor, though other departments had also played their due roles in all the activities (infrastructure, social development and economic support programmes), the beneficiaries were involved by and large. The neighbourhood committees, Basti committees, Mahila mandals, Youth clubs stand as evidence to this. However the initial enthusiasm evaporated with time, as the external fundings started melting away with time (it is not unexpected because everybody in the process knew, on day one, the duration of the project assistance). All the time the UCD staff who were involved in the implementation, over played their roles and thereby the communities "Dependency" on the system was never ending. No sincere attempts were made, by the line departments to create adequate capacity among the leaders so that they could bear the torch at the end of the day with self-confidence. Though "training" for enpowerment and capacity building was an integral component of the programme, they were never taken note of and implemented seriously.

In those 510 slums, where infrastructure was created, much is still intact but the maintenance is poor. As the notified slums were the targets for development in isolation, many unrecognised slums, inhabited by urban poor are left as they are, without any developmental programme. This target approach needs revision. Thus the programmes could not cater to the needs of "urban poor" per se but helped slum dwellers. The slums are also pampered by local political leaders, as they are their solid vote banks. The protection has gone to such an extent, that those fully developed slums that need no more "free services" and are capable of paying for and buying services are denotified by Government. But within a short period they were again "renotified" as slums. The number of slums was 408 (1997) and their number has again shot back to 811 (1998). Now in 1999 there are hardly 150 new slums which need to be improved and serviced. Unless corrective administrative measures are taken by Government, the slum improvement will be a never ending work and a drain on the exchequer of Municipal Corporation of Hyderabad. They should pass a legislation that beyond, say 2002 A.D., there would be no more slums that would be taken up for development. Now it is high time to stop spending time, money and efforts on physical development of slums (old or new) but concentrate on 'Human Resource Development' by adopting suitable, context appropriate, locally acceptable Information, Education and Communication (I.E.C.) methods, which will go a long way in programme sustenance.

The task of slum improvement is so gigantic and continuous that it would be difficult for any single agency to handle — finances, personnel etc. This would be more difficult through mobilising internal resources of local government organisations. The service delivery has to be regularised, by MCH by raising local resources. Once the process is set in motion with full involvement of people, it can be an effective programme.

For example, in the beginning, UCD was having very skeletal staff till 1983. Before HSIP came in a big way, the UCD was playing its role, more as a facilitator and a catalyst. The involvement of the people was more and any department's role was minimal — at best advisory and supportive. With this partnership approach UCD could do wonders for 16 years and implemented many programmes. But with ODA funds, the budget has gone up several times and spending was the main motto. The service spirit, community involvement got the back seat and the contractors gained upper hand. Even a parallel UCD was run for "ODA programmes" implementation. After the closure of HSIP-III stage, the present UCD's budget has come down to Rs. 106 lakhs per year, of which 85 per cent goes to salaries of the staff. The staff pattern remained the same but the activities of the staff became multifarious. That is the present status of UCD. Now efforts should be made to strengthen its hands and get back to its past glory.

It is high time to involve the stake holders into the fold (74th amendment — Maha Nagara Palika bill) of various programmes that were initiated by UCD and other departments. They all should converge and be managed by people themselves with the single goal of "sustenance". Otherwise the system is likely to collapse under its own weight. An earnest beginning should be made on a clean slate — to impart extension, education, training by selecting appropriate communication methods, by qualified, trained, experienced persons. At the apex level there can be an "Empowerment Promotion Centre" or "Swayam Shakti Sadhana Kendram" with branches at circle levels. This should have active kendras at slum level. The locally selected and trained volunteers (M & F) should train people — based on their demands and get themselves trained periodically.

Some of the key issues that need immediate/better attention are :

1. Create enough opportunities that provide assured livelihood and improve quality of life of poor.
2. Encourage the participation of stakeholders, at all levels of the programme — planning, implementation, monitoring, contribution (physical and financial) and evaluation. The programmes should be demand driven rather than supply oriented.
3. By raising the levels of literacy of men, women and children simultaneously, the most important Human resource development (H.R.D.) component, the process of transfer of assets, maintenance and sustenance of programmes can be assured/guaranteed. Adult education

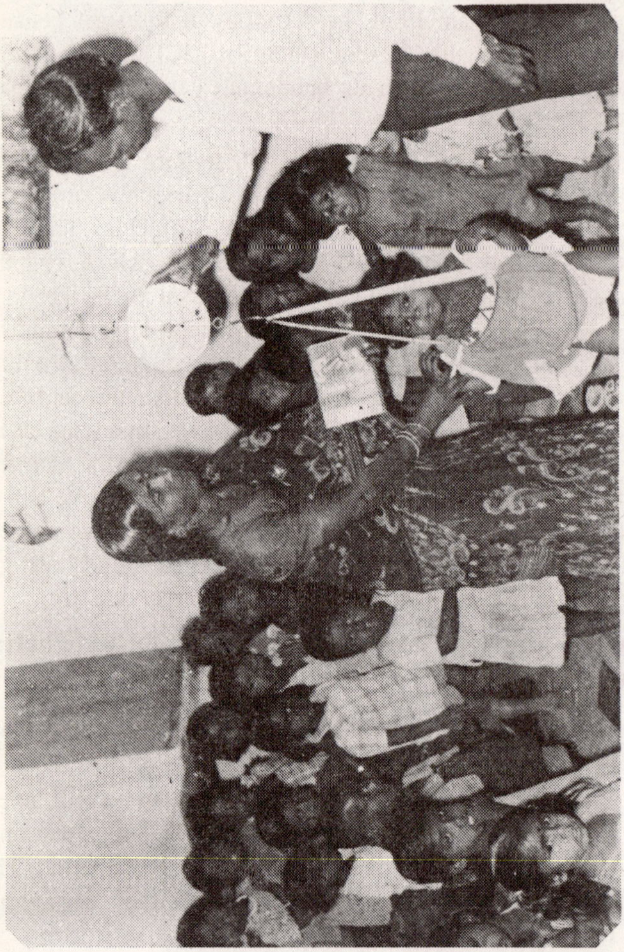

GROWTH MONITORING BY NEIGHBOURHOOD COMMITTEE

classes by local instructors should be on a continuing basis, as literacy is the pre-condition for the formation, management of thrift and credit (women) groups (Bangladesh experience). This would go a long way in sustaining many programmes : like cost recovery, payment for services, low dependence on the existing systems etc.

4. Another important facet of H.R.D. is health. Unless the society is disease-free, people cannot think of any other responsibility. Hence on the health front, the Government, MCH (UCD) should (with the help of IPP VIII) help people by creating awareness about public health, hygiene preventive/curative aspects. The health delivery system should be streamlined to provide qualified medical advice as well as medicines to all the urban poor in their locality, at times suitable to them. Just by constructing health posts (physical building), the governments responsibility will not cease. There should be regular and periodical "monitoring" by the authorities, followed by stern action for the lapses. Barefoot doctors and medicine banks by Non governmental organisations (NGOs) can be tried.

Now the people are ready to pay for the services if the quality is assured and up to the mark, even to a Government agency — as they are already paying to private medical practitioners in their neighbourhood. So, services can be charged and "cost recovery" may not be difficult in the context of the poor.

It is imperative to create a "needle eye" in the system, like "Urban Poverty Eradication Cell" (UPEC) at MCH, headed by an I.A.S. officer where all departments concerned should have their representatives. Though it looks "duplication", it is a must to cut short red-tapism and ensure quick delivery of services to the urban poor. In the service delivery to the urban poor there can be a partnership approach (replacing the earlier, loan, grant, margin money, subsidy and beneficiary contribution — finally without any accountability) where the local recognised NGO, with appreciable track record, can be the main actor, catalyst, helping the beneficiary to receive the programme from the Government with the least hurdles. The same NGO can train the people to manage, monitor to sustain the programme on their own and as their own.

22

Suitable Approaches and Strategies

Social Mobilisation and Group Formation

Unless poor people who have strength in their sheer numbers, do not unite, they cannot achieve economic growth or social justice, especially in our societies characterised by rigid social hierarchic and authoritarian structures, obstructing the opportunity for equal and just acquisition of resources and privileges. The concept of thrift and credit groups can be replicated on a large scale. The envisaged programme should promote the welfare of the people through the principle of self-reliance and self-respect. The new process envisages "operation by people and cooperation by Government" implying participatory approach by Government — not by people. In a systematic way, the capacity of the people can be built and at the event of withdrawal donor agency, people will be well prepared to take over and sustain the programmes successfully. The approach of the groups should be dead serious. They should be professional in approach and incredibly methodical in attitude. From time to time depending on the needs and demands of the community, the leadership should search for additional options and innovations.

Creation of social funds within slums, as a self-generating and sustaining fund, to attend to the maintenance of common physical and institutional resources, to meet the emergencies that arise in the community and to provide assistance to the individual households to meet emergency expenditure related to personal accidents, fire, sudden illness, periodic unemployment etc., should be a part of capacity building.

The groups (other than women's thrift and credit groups)

should be formed for a group of slums, with large organisational dimensions in terms of Participation, Decision Making, Accountability etc.

Measurable Performance/Outcome Indicators

The envisaged programmes involving continuous social mobilisation and participatory process requires an inbuilt Monitoring and Evaluation (M&E) process to ensure realisation of the expected performance and outcome. Some of them are :

* Economic benefits	* Awareness creation	* Skill development
* Savings	* Cultural values	* Economic/Social development
* Investment	* Gender equality	
* Asset creation	* Self-reliance	* Generating internal leadership
* Social benefits	* Strong local groups	
* Distributional Equity		* Multiplication

The overall development is expected to be underlined by the increased critical consciousness, empowerment and self-respect which are the three cornerstones on which the edifice of sustenance can be built safely.

Observations

* the departments involved in delivery of urban services include town planning, engineering, health, education, welfare etc. but their tasks are too many and capabilities are limited. Most of them are burdened with routine administrative work than with their professional work. Though most of them undergo training within the country or abroad, the sad part is that they are not continued in the same post but transferred after their return from training.
* Their activities are monitored by commissioner (MCH) regularly and hence there is no room for overlapping and "inter-agency" coordination which is possible.

* UCD works exclusively for the slum development, with separate budget and personnel of course under the overall vision of additional commissioner, and in coordination with related departments in providing infrastructure, environmental improvement, socio-economic development, preventive health and other programmes.
* The finances appear to be inadequate. Still the expenditure on salaries of the staff itself is very high (80%) leaving meagre amounts for activities.
* Though Rs. 50 lakhs was earmarked for 1996-97 for post project sustenance, it was not released for 2 years.
* These departments are working with a project/programme based approach. All the departmental personnel were given training abroad by O.D.A. for service provision with a community oriented approach. But the limitation now is non-availability of funds though expertise is available.
* In case inter-departmental disputes, if any, arise in implementing the programmes, they are solved at the standing committee level or by commissioner (MCH).
* When once the programme implementation is transferred to C.B.Os/NHCs, monitoring, guiding, supervision will be the responsibility of various agencies — maintenance and sustenance will be transferred to community itself.
* For successful public-private partnership in delivering services to urban poor, a few items can be identified and processes can be monitored by UCD on the lines of "Build own" — "Operate-Transfer".

✪

(23)

S.W.O.T. Analysis — U.C.D. Department

A. Strengths

* Very long and valuable experience built over decades with the communities.
* Tangible Community approach/involvement.
* As facilitator/catalyst, UCD has been playing unique role by making people to take decisions, maintain programmes.
* Low budget and limited personnel : Cost effective (?).
* Sustenance of the projects by people has been made easy.
* Continuation of the programmes by community after the withdrawal of UCD is a part of the plan.

B. Weaknesses

* Right type of leadership to direct the programme. No authority to report to Commissioner, M.C.H.
* Always playing secondary roles ignoring the legitimate ones.
* Cannot implement any programme on its own — only through different departments, more of co-ordination.
* Presently insufficient not — right type of staff and budget.
* Staff diverted to other jobs like bill collection, administrative work leading to lack of concentration and follow-up.

C. Opportunities

* Can transform its entire future course if transfer of programmes to CBOs is intensified and it becomes an NGO network based activity.
* Can improve further its role in planning, implementation, and monitoring of several programmes through community participation.
* Can play important role by making use of the rapport established over decades with communities in their capacity building (Group formation, Thrift, Credit etc.).
* With more involvement in regular, refresher and periodical training programmes, CBOs can be qualified for empowerment.

D. Threats

* People with right aptitude and ability should be appointed.
* Senior staff needs encouragement and should be allowed to work in the same line. Encourage activities or ideas in the field which are demand driven by the community.
* Staff are being diverted to other jobs — delearning process.
* Rapport established with community over decades should be used as a treasure and with its help, base can be formed to sustain and handover the programmes to the community at a later date.
* Political interference.
* Traditional/Natural leaders, vested interests coming in the way of the formation of CBO, NHC, CDS on objective criteria.

24

Poverty Alleviation Programme for Urban Poor : Co-ordinated Effort by MCH and UCD

Housing

There are several schemes (now may be merged with new schemes under new names) which provide housing to urban poor : Hyderabad District Housing Scheme, E.W.S. Housing Scheme, Indira Awaas Yojana, Shelter upgradation programme etc. sponsored/ funded by different agencies like District Collector, MCH, APUD and HC, HUDCO, etc.

Civic Amenities

Like Roads, Community Halls, S.S. flooring, garbage removal, drinking water, sewerage, low cost sanitation, street lights, latest national slum development programme, Adarsh Bastis etc. They are provided by MCH, QQDA, HUDA, H.M.W.S.S.B., UNICEF, APSEB.

Income Generation Activities (I.G.A.)

They are many as in SJSRY, Cobblers Development, Women Development, CMEY, DWCRA, SETWIN etc. by various state government corporations.

For Women and Child Development

Balwadi, Anganwadi, Girl Child Protection Scheme, Back to School, Balajyothi (rehabilitation of child labour), shelter for street children etc., are sponsored by MCH, UCD, Social Welfare Departments.

WOMEN AT CARPENTRY WORK

* In addition Aksharajyothi, continuing education. Adult education classes are being conducted by District Collector, MCH, UCD, Adult education department.
* Formation of Thrift and Credit Groups, empowerment centres, Training Programmes are being taken up by MCH/UCD/NABARD, Indira Mahila Kosh, etc. Mahila Janma Bhoomi (May 1 week) was an attempt in this direction.

Health and Nutrition

Health and Nutrition of the urban poor is taken care of by Urban Welfare (UFW) Schemc, C.S.W. Scheme, S.N.P. IPP VIII, National Maternity Benefit Scheme. They are operated by MCH, UCD, Health Department, etc.

Andhra Pradesh State Government has newly introduced some innovative programmes like Adarana, Apadbhandu, Mundadugu, etc. for the welfare of the urban poor.

Thus it can be seen that there are more than 25 programmes implemented by various departments for the welfare of the urban poor. It is possible that some of the programmes may overlap. So, the need of the hour is to bring them under a single authority, to coordinate various programmes, avoid duplication, optimise the utilisation of the funds/resources, to meet the need of the urban poor. This task can be better done through C.B.Os which know their needs and demands. By imparting proper training to the leaders, the task can be handed over to the people themselves with the government agencies relegated behind the scene — to play supervisory and advisory role. Then the services will have quality and be cost effective too.

PART II

GROWTH OF UCD OVER TIME

UCD was basically conceived as a programme for towns and cities with large population. Parallel to this, with cooperation and support from UNICEF, the government at the Centre initiated Small and Medium Town Development programme (SMTD) in selected towns, having population of less than 1 lakh emphasizing infrastructure development. People's involvement was also suggested but not much insisted on as in UCD as there was no special motivating force within the local body.

1

Urban Basic Services (UBS)

Again with UNICEF assistance, the programme of Urban Basic Services was initiated for several towns with the sharing pattern kept at 40 : 40 : 20 between UNICEF, Govt. of India and State Government. But in Andhra Pradesh (A.P.) and Orissa where I was the Project Officer for this programme, it was decided to involve the beneficiary local bodies also and so sought for 25 per cent contribution from them too. This made the local bodies possess the programme as their own and thus pay better attention to it.

The community structures were very well streamlined in this programme straight from Town Level Monitoring Committee right down to neighbourhood groups at the community level with systematic linkages.

There is adequate representation for the Neighbourhood Committees at the T.L.M.C. (Town level monitoring committee) level to ensure close monitoring and approve realistic community based activities.

Community Organizers were also appointed in all towns at the rate of one for every 2,000 families taking the precaution that half of them are women.

Delegation of Power

Community development is a process in which the local communities are motivated or a conscious decision is initiated by the authorities to delegate or transfer responsibilities to people and thus initiate a welcome beginning of enabling people to manage their affairs in their own humble way. Does the bureaucracy or the existing political structure get ready to relinquish minimum powers to community based organisations or do they feel they do not wish to lose their importance and always want people to crave for mercy and help, however simple and silly it might be? Will it be offered or has it to be demanded? The Community Worker has a role to play in both situations.

Local Body Stake

To insist on the local body also to meet part of the budget cost was opposed earlier by different agencies. Wherever there is no local body contribution, the community as well as the project workers begin to feel that UBS is a Government and UNICEF programme and the local body is only used as medium to implement it and so they show no accountability to the local body concerned. This again made the local body feel that UBS is its step child and began to devote less attention to its implementation.

Financial support for staff is given by UNICEF for two years *in toto* in a five year plan and the Government is asked to find its own resources to support the staff for the remaining three years. To make the Government committed for the total period, right from beginning, 40 per cent of their share is sought for the total period of 5 years. As far as UNICEF is concerned, it makes no difference. It was a matter of discomfort for Government which has to plan for the staff budget right from the beginning. But it ensured full complement of staff in position for the total implementation period.

UBS as one understands is a flexible programme and need not be stereotyped. The innovative modifications made at Local/State level in terms of budget, composition of NHCs, staff recruitment etc. have a lot of bearing not only on success of the programme but also on its continuity.

UBS is a low budgeted programme and so to make it successful the Community Organisers had to organize, educate and motivate the communities in an intensive way to make it beautiful and impressive though small.

The UBS Programme Undertakes Activities

- to improve the socio-economic and physical environment of the urban poor.
- to make urban poor aware of the programmes available to them and to motivate them to seek assistance to improve their conditions.
- to organise neighbourhood groups and motivate them to actively participate in implementing their own programmes.

Community Participation through Neighbourhood Planning

Community participation is one of the cardinal elements for successful implementation of UBS Programme adopting a community development approach.

Women are given special attention by UNICEF especially in their critical role as mothers. It was initially limited to maternity and child health services. Later, it was extended to activities connected with education, literacy, better home management, improved child development, appropriate technology to relieve women from daily drudgery, pre-school activities, income generation support and leadership development. All these social and connected services for mother and child development culminated in the demand for more status and respect for women in the society as a whole.

Neighbourhood Committee (NHC) is a practical, though difficult answer through which small groups of about 200 women can be empowered in any given slum community. Minimum needs in terms of guidance, financial support and regular flow of services to improve the life of women and children have of course to be provided in time to them at their initiative.

In a Neighbourhood Committee approach, small groups are formed with women members from every 15 to 30 families. These women select a representative from amongst themselves who is designated as Resident Community Volunteer (RCV). They together form the Neighbourhood Committee (NHC). The RCV is the spokeswoman and at the same time accountable for her small group of 15 to 30 families. She promotes a two-way communication by which the grass-root problems at group level are well brought out in the NHC discussions and the decisions and goals of the total committee are effectively communicated to her group to facilitate easy accomplishment.

They have their set objectives with emphasis on mother and child development, home and environmental sanitation and extra income generation opportunities for women. These are all consolidated into a Mini Action Plan on the strength of which the town authorities release some imprest amount through which they become the implementers and managers of their own programme with support from the local body and other agencies.

Through this NHC approach there is good prospect for raising the status of women both within the family and the community.

2

New and Novel Approaches in UBS

I was constantly on tours and during my routine trips I came across some new and novel approaches, attempted by different Neighbourhood Committees. I thought they would be of guidance to field workers and so I prepared some Case Studies/Illustrations which are detailed below.

Do not Stick to the Beaten Track — Look for Innovations

In one NHC of Chintala Cheruvu in Suryapet, the women invited me to sit on the only available chair but I was reluctant and stood with the group of about 30 women, councilors and youths for over two hours near the newly constructed community workshed. There are two neem trees and a heap of stones around it.

"We have this problem of sitting together because the community workshed is often occupied by either a balwadi or a sewing centre." To this statement by some members, there was prompt suggestion from another member : "Why do we not have a community platform around and underneath these trees and another constructed in front of the balwadi which can provide sitting accommodation for all of us on occasions like this?" Another idea that came was to request the Municipality to provide a mercury vapour lamp in front of the balwadi. A woman of the adjacent house agreed to put a bulb outside temporarily to run adult literacy centre for women in the evenings. Where there is a will, one will find the way! In all these inputs, the assistance from UBS is only the cost of material. The community has no hesitation to take care of the "Shramdan" part.

Free Ventilators Causing Problems

The NHC member, Smt. Lakshmamma, is in-charge of sanitation in Chintala Cheruvu of Suryapet. After the beneficiaries were selected by the committee, she took the initiative to procure 60 ventilators and distributed them without the mediation of the RCVs representing different groups. Since it is a free item there was a big crowd which led to chaos.

She committed two mistakes :

- She did not insist on the beneficiary to excavate the wall and make space to accommodate the ventilator before it was supplied.
- She did not enlist the co-operation of the group RCVs who would have facilitated this at their neighbourhood group level.

These mistakes were unintentional but they marred the friendly atmosphere. COs must anticipate such things in advance and offer necessary guidance to RCVs. A similar situation may arise while distributing plants, latrine closets or slabs or channels for drains.

This had resulted in the unpleasant task of taking back ventilators from some of the beneficiaries. The programme was also delayed.

Balwadi Workers

Balwadi or pre-school activity is very popular in towns. Teen-aged girls who have studied upto matric are often chosen to run the balwadi schools. However after a period of time, their enthusiasm and zeal wanes out on account of the nature of work and the remuneration they receive from the NHC. It may provide an avocation for the unemployed girls, but it is at the same time affecting their future career as they think it is a dead-end job. This method is absolutely wrong. We must encourage such girls for vocational training or higher education offering necessary assistance from UBS.

For young mothers, aged over 25 years, with one or two children, this pre-school work would be a useful supplemental income activity. They have patience and know how to take care of children. They are married and already settled. With suitable training, they can be efficient worker commanding adequate respect and reputation from the neighbourhood. It does not matter if they are educated only up to sixth standard. They must be active and dynamic.

Can we gradually transform the present situation motivating NHCs to make necessary changes? In the towns I visited, there were only two unmarried girls amongst 23 balwadi workers, the rest being housewives. This type of situation may prevail in other towns also.

No Bar on Age for Learning

Mrs. Jasti Chittemma, 60 years, is working as an ayah in a balwadi. She was motivated to take up reading and writing when she observed tiny tots learning alphabets and numbers. That was not all. She thought "I am learning something everyday at the balwadi. Why not I transmit this to some others like myself who are illiterate?" Now she makes it a habit to learn new things at the balwadi. Before she returns home she calls on four or five of her neighbours and tells them what she learnt in the balwadi that day. This she is continuing since April 1986, till what date? I do not know. Can you imagine the number of literates turned out by Mrs. Chittemma?

Creches

During my field trip I chose to sit on the platform near a small hut. The elders of the house went to the field. There were only three children — two girls aged 9 and 7 and one boy aged 3 years. When I initiated an informal chat, Gandamma, the eldest girl said I have to feed my brother and sister. Then I go out with the cattle. My sister takes care of our brother until we all come back."

Then an old lady of about 60 years, Savaramma, came to us with her grandson in arms (aged two years). When asked what she does all day, comes the prompt response : "I care for this boy the whole day when his parents go out for work". When asked, "Instead of just one, can you take care of about ten children if the parents give you some food for the children and show some accommodation along with toys, cradles etc.? You can also get some remuneration for taking care of these children. Can you take

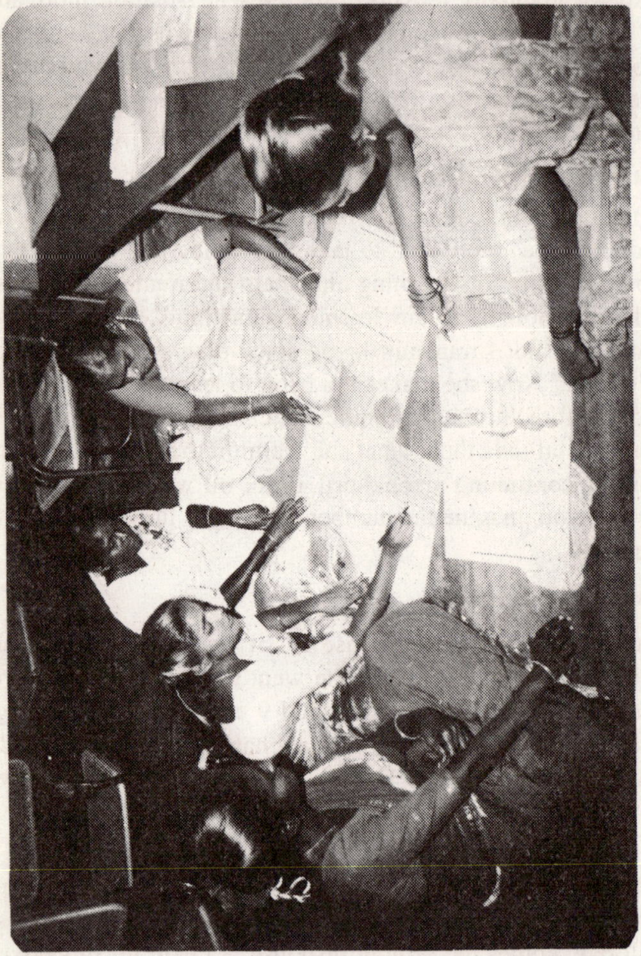

GROUP WORK IN COMMUNITY HEALTH VOLUNTEERS TRAINING

care of and also don't mind washing them when the children pass urine or stools?" The reply was quick : "They will be treated as my grand-children and I don't mind doing anything for them. If I am provided with soap, powder and water, I can give them a bath, keep them fresh and hand them over to the parents when they come back."

Here is an answer to our problem of organizing Creches. There is a solution if only we think seriously about it and observe the practical realities of life! In the meeting at the Municipal Office on the previous day, we spoke of remuneration, accommodation and other aspects. But we could not come out with a tangible solution.

Community Health Volunteers (CHVs) and Drugs Replenishment

The lady CHVs, after undergoing a 10-day training course, are given a first aid kit. Their services are no doubt well appreciated by the respective NHCs. But it all ended in the first aid kit getting depleted in no time.

What is the answer to ensure a continuing activity? This must be found by the NHC itself. And it did. Medicines worth Rs. 100 were purchased from NHC funds on the assurance that the CHV collects a minimum of Rs. 50 through a "hundi" and pays it back to NHC. Next time she agrees to collect the full amount from her patients.

This is possible with every CHV. She has knowledge of Primary Health Care and First Aid. "Knowledge is power and power should lead to respect". "Service to needy persons is service to God." All CHVs should ensure it as a continuing activity and see that the First Aid kit does not get empty. This will help boost her morale and standing in the community.

Income Generation and Skills Improvement Training for Women

Some bureaucrats feel that the poor are helpless and cannot do anything. They also think that Rs. 200 or Rs. 300 (I am referring to 1980's) can hardly be of any use to the poor. But it is seen that this sum comes as a boon to the person, who has high potential and initiative. Many women are benefited by the petty loans extended by NHCs. Repayment is also assured as they are recommended by the concerned RCV who represents the group of 20 women. No bad debts! We saw the loans being utilized for setting up petty grocery shops, tea stalls, eggs counters, sale of broiler chicken, preparation of leaf-mats, leaf-plates, brooms, hair-wigs, sweets, vegetables, raising kitchen garden etc. These petty occupations bring in money for daily living. Families are able to get rid of the exorbitant interest hitherto paid to private vendors, which is as high as Rs. 10 per hundred per day.

Sewing Centres

It is conceived as a skills training centre and the syllabus is to be covered in eight months time, followed by a test. Presuming that there will not be more than three batches of trainees in each NHC, the sewing centre in any NHC should not continue for more than two years. In case there are any more trainees left, the centre has to be shifted along with the worker, machine and other equipment and the girls who are yet to be trained have to be advised to go to the nearby centre.

In Suryapet, I came across a sewing teacher who used to charge Rs. 300 to train a candidate in all sewing work catering to domestic needs in just over three months' time. This is now transformed into a UBS sewing centre where no fee is collected. By this we have perhaps curbed a local initiative which should not have been the case. The NHC could have picked up some poor persons and helped them by providing some subsidy to learn from the already existing institution.

The NHC must know that the sewing machine used for training will not remain there forever. It must be motivated to have its own, on a matching contribution basis.

Points to be Noted

(a) The UBS-sponsored sewing centre cannot be a permanent institution in any NHC for more than two years.

(b) Reorganize the sewing centres to have at least two machines each and ensure that the number of centres are reduced.

(c) Do not disrupt or damage the ongoing activities as was experienced in Suryapet. Think and see how best you can help the NHC members make use of them.

(d) Stimulate the NHCs to buy a machine on a contribution basis for the benefit of trained candidates before the centre is shifted.

Coming to the Aid of a Rickshaw Puller

A Municipal Commissioner assured one Rikshaw puller that he will secure a loan for a rickshaw but there is no margin money and subsidy coming forth from other governmental agencies.

My question : "Why all that, can you not explore and do it yourself?"

Ans : "Margin money required is about Rs. 500. A rickshaw puller mobilizes his resources and opens an account with Rs. 250. The NHC sanctions a loan of Rs. 250 to his wife and remits the same into the account. The loan is sanctioned in the joint names of husband and wife. The loan taken from NHC is repaid in three instalments. The NHC takes the responsibility for repayment of the bank loan and ensures it through review in NHC meetings."

The NHC says that it is a workable solution and in each of the twenty odd committees, they promised to start with four rickshaws. They said "if we wait for margin money and subsidy, we will never be able to do anything.''

(Can we try a similar method, whether it is for a sewing machine, TV or some other equipment costing Rs. 2,000 to Rs. 4,000?)

NHC Meetings

Proceedings of these meetings should facilitate learning about correct procedures. These meetings must be seriously taken and the resolutions made therein should act as instruments to solicit services from UBS and other agencies on a partnership basis. All RCVs must be made active participants in periodic meetings, which can be made more meaningful by :

- the Community Organiser actively participating in all these meetings for at least two hours. This may be held on a fixed day and time of every month.
- Stimulating RCVs to come out with their experiences

DISTRIBUTION OF SMOKELESS CHULLAHS

and successes in the tasks assigned to each of them. This means review of last month's accomplishments and plans for next month in every field, by every RCV, *viz.*, Universal immunization, sanitation, balwadi, income generation activities and so on, as detailed in the objectives of the NHC.

- Making it a closed cell meeting at an isolated place only for RCVs and Community Organiser.
- Stimulating each RCV to tell something about her group. To make this more meaningful the RCV should sit with her group members once prior to the NHC meeting. (I fear this aspect of interaction is not given due importance by the project staff.) The Committee has to review the expenditure of the previous month including loans collected and to be disbursed.
- Approving the expenditure of the previous month including loans collected and to be disbursed.
- Approving the expenditure statement to be sent to Municipality etc.

The CO must act as a friend, philosopher and guide to the groups intervening in the discussions and initiating the work by himself only when necessary. Every woman must know who is her RCV. Every RCV should know very well about her Neighbourhood Group members.

It does not matter if the NHCs are few. But quality-wise, they must prove successful. The CO can do a lot in this regard.

Development Register

The information that you have in the development register must lead to continuing action and this has to be seriously examined by CO's at every stage. For instance if there is a list of children in Balwadis, it must reflect who are the neglected ones in the pre-school activity, and what remedial action the NHC has thought of. If growth monitoring is done, what follow-up action is suggested for the malnourished? Suitable columns and sufficient space is necessary for each item in the register.

Resident Community Volunteers (RCVs) Work to Achieve National Plan of Action goals

1. Ensure every new born child is fully immunized by age of 11 months.
2. Ensure every pregnant woman attends at least 3-4 antenatal clinics and gets and consumes the iron-folic tablets daily, and gets her 2 doses of tetanus vaccination.
3. Ensures all small children aged 9 months to 36 months get their vitamin A syrup — 5 doses at 6 monthly intervals.
4. Ensures every home is using only iodized salt to protect the mother and children from iodine deficiency disorders.
5. Ensure ORS is available and used correctly for treatment of dehydration due to diarrhea especially for children.
6. Ensure there are no severely malnourished children of below 2 years in her area.
7. Ensure all children aged 5/6 — 10 years are in primary school.
8. Ensure that all children in school stay in school until they complete at least 5th standard.
9. Ensure that every family has its own latrine as a priority. If it is feasible, she has atleast a clean community latrine in the close vicinity.

All Women NHC

Considering the cultural backwardness and oldage traditions, only women were chosen as RCVs by community groups and thus the Neighbourhood Committees in A.P. and Orissa consist only of women unlike in other States. This made the NHCs more emphatic on women and child activities and also made the women vocal and demanding. This situation was all together different in other States where the NHCs have men also as members who are more vocal and dominant. So the women remained where they were earlier both socially and economically. In those days, when we visited some projects in other States and wanted to have a dialogue with the NHC members, only men RCVs participated and they said women RCVs are busy with domestic work.

There was severe criticism against A.P. and Orissa for having only women in NHCs earlier. But later the Government and UNICEF realized it is the right step to make women come to the forefront in all community development issues. Now NHCs all over the country are having only women as its members since NHGs (Neighbourhood Groups) were all advised to choose only women as their representative RCVs.

Some Thoughts on UBS

Some NHC members are still not very clear about their roles and they throw the entire responsibility on the Convenor/Secretary. The COs must participate in at least one NHC meeting once a month. The NHC members, each holding a separate task, must be helped to know their role well *e.g.*, a NHC member in-charge of balwadi should be aware of the number of children between 3-6 years, attendance and drop-outs, fees collected, position of dues, teacher's punctuality, accounting, what is required from the Municipality, etc. Improvement of quality and efficiency of NHCs is very important and each NHC member should be aware of and well versed with the contents of the NHC registers.

The NHC Convenor is responsible for the cheque book, cash book and NHC registers. COs are making entries in the registers which is not correct. UBS is more an educational process. The CO must teach the NHC members how to handle these tasks.

In one town I found the NHC cheque book and pass book are kept with the Community Organiser. I questioned the Convenor as to why it is so? She said that her house is a small hut amenable for theft or fire. I saw one nose stud and ear stud as ornaments on her and I jovially questioned "why do you not keep them with the CO. She caught the point and assured they will be with her only in future.

In one town in a particular State, in the capacity of a Consultant, I had a review with the Project staff. The records revealed, there are the NHCs, RCVs and so on. This is wonderful. Then I said, I would like to visit some NHCs at random and have discussions with the groups. Then the truth came out, that these Committees are only on record; but the story in the field is totally different.

Satisfying the bosses and achieving the targets through paper work is an inexcusable mistake and it is only deceiving the poor.

Without explaining the purpose the COs at times get the signatures of the NHC Convenor. This is highly irregular. When a cheque is drawn, the NHC Convenor even in the absence of the CO, should be able to say the cheque is drawn for a specific purpose and expenditure is shown in the register.

Expenditure register at NHC level should be entered in the local language by the member. The format has to be simple as suggested in the NHC guide book.

UBS — It is a Part of Local Body

UCD is a programme implemented by the Municipality which means the Chairman, the Councilors and the Municipal Commissioner have a say in it. The contention of a few staff members that it has no connection with the Municipality is absolutely wrong. But one should impress upon the elected representatives that they should not interfere with the democratic process of grass-root planning and management.

The effort to innovate and implement new activities is to be intensified by the COs. Their visits to communities should be more purposeful.

Exchange Visits

Exchange of ideas and exposure to new thoughts go a long way in making the women in the NHCs intellectually rich. Such acts expand their horizons of vision and thinking, in addition to giving them the much needed courage and boldness in the traditional society. There are several UBS towns with thousands of RCVs. The women from one town were asked to go to another town and be the guests of Committee members there for a week and come back. After a week's interval the groups from the other towns repeat the process and come back. The wealth of wisdom they get by these Exchange visits is invaluable. In such cases, it is not a waste for the project to meet the minimum travel expenses and a pocket allowance of Rs. 20 a day may be allowed to both the hosts and guests, who are poor women and who should not be burdened financially. Imagine the camaraderie and the spirit of integration it can build up between different communities, towns and even amongst States. In an International Exchange Visit or Study Tour, what is invested on one person can suffice for hundreds of RCVs in this way and the results will be fantastic.

Sharing of Responsibility

The aim of project staff should be to keep the NHCs active at every movement. All members of NHC must find their role meaningful. So sharing of responsibility of recognition of talent is a must. They are all economically backward but they still volunteered to play an active role in the Community Development Programmes. Every RCV must be entrusted with a specific task. In the monthly NHC meeting, she must be encouraged to speak of her achievements or problems to the group. No one should be made to feel big in the Committee. If one RCV is incharge of preschool, she must say every thing about it. Like that each RCV can be volunteered to take up one specific task like immunization, skills centre, first-aid, sanitation, cultural activities, water supply, tree plantation, community hall, nutrition, training, loans and thrift, etc.

The effort should be to make these meetings very systematic and regular, at the same time interesting and through this, democratic leadership qualities should be imbibed amongst the members. Each NHC must have one meeting every month and the date and time should be fixed in advance. People's participation should always be the main focus. Then RCVs will be very active.

Encourage and Respect RCVs

The RCVs have no remuneration since they have volunteered to do a particular task. But there must be adequate incentives created to recognise and appreciate their services and to encourage special skills and talents. Three or four RCVs in each NHC may be selected every year for meritorious service. Competitions may be held in various activities centered round women and children like cutting, embroidery, elocution, best student, best hygienic habits, drawing competition, songs, mono-actions, mimicry, fancy dress, best social work, bravery, eating competition, best maintained kitchen, toilets etc. Utility articles of a moderate cost should be given as prizes. Sufficient provision is necessary every year in the Municipal budget for this activity.

By giving interview whenever solicited and offering a chair or seat to a poor woman, the officer loses nothing; but gets a lot of mileage in his task accomplishment. She will not forget it so easily and be grateful forever. This should not be forgotten by the Community Development Workers, whatever level they may be. Inculcate the habit of calling as many as possible by name and with utmost love and respect. One must realise that everybody has got worth and he/she has got some ability to contribute and make the programme a success. To be a successful Community Worker, one must be of excellent character and behaviour with no vices or corrupt attitudes and he/she must build up such a reputation that he/she always gives the right direction and guidance with no motive behind. One has to go a long way to get such a reputation; but it takes no time to get it nullified with a single act of misdeed.

3

Urban Basic Services Programme in Andhra Pradesh

Three years after implementing UBS in Andhra Pradesh and Orissa, Sri Dev D. Chopra, Zonal Chief in Hyderabad and Sri Leo Fonseka, Chief of Urban Development in UNICEF in Delhi suggested that we should understand the impact and utility of our UBS experience. Mr. Ganesan, retired Hindu Correspondent agreed to take up the assignment and visited all the towns. He was generally very happy with the response and enthusiasm shown by the poor to UBS and some of his observations are indicated below.

Mumtaz Begum on Urban Basic Services

"We were like bonded labour, always confined to the four walls of the house. Like frogs in the well, we did not know what was existing and happening outside. It is only after the introduction of the Programme of Urban Basic Services that we have come to know what the world is like." It was Mrs. Mumtaz Begum, sewing instructress at the Gymkhanaguda slum in Bhongir town of Nalgonda district who minced no words in describing the gains of the UBS programme. There was no vagueness in her declaration. In clear-cut words she echoed the feelings of a dozen women who were surrounding her.

"We were not even allowed to see movies. We never stirred out of the house. Now, we have learnt about immunization and sanitation. We are sending our young children to the Balwadi School. We hold meetings at the community hall and attend training classes. We want to install a television set." It looked as if Mrs. Mumtaz Begum and others like her were eager to learn as quickly as possible, all that they could not over the last two decades.

That, to me, seemed to be one of the great achievements of the UBS programme. It has brought about a qualitative change in the lives of people like Mrs. Mumtaz Begum. Is that not a measure of the programme being successful, of it achieving its purpose?

Mrs. Venkatamma and Kamala on Creche

Mrs. Venkatamma, mother of a two-year-old child, volunteered the information that she was leaving her child in the creche since the last one month while going out to work as an agricultural labourer. "Till last month, I used to leave the child with my neighbours but they have also to be away." Mrs. Kamala, handing over her one-year-old child to Lachmamma, pointed out that she used to take the child also to the fields. "I used to be afraid that grazing cattle might trample the child or some insects bite him. Now, I am able to concentrate on my work. I come at 4.00 p.m. to take the child home.

Mrs. B. Ramnarsamma on Community Hall

Mrs. B. Ramnarsamma, Convenor of the Neighbourhood Committee, said that while the UBS authorities gave Rs. 10,000 for the community hall, the women of the area had undertaken all the manual work connected with the construction of the community hall.

"If we had engaged labour for the purpose, it would have cost us not less than Rs. 5,000." They were now planning to construct a circular platform around a big peepal tree in front of the community hall. "It will cost us Rs. 8,000. We will get Rs. 5,000 from the UBS and the rest will be contribution from us either in cash or in shape of labour."

The Convenor pointed out that the women were not in the habit of taking their disputes to court. "The disputes are referred to the Panchayat consisting of women. Their decisions are accepted *in toto*. Once the platform is ready, this panchayat will meet here." The panchayat handles only women's cases.

The members of the Neighbourhood Committees are now clamouring for a TV. "But, before the TV is installed, we must get the ground paved with stone. Otherwise, our clothes will get soiled if we sit on the bare earth." That was certainly an indication of their having become aware of the need for cleanliness.

The area was once dirty with sewage water running onto the lanes, stagnating and creating a cesspool, to be the breeding ground for mosquitoes. Now, waste water is rarely to be seen. There is no slush anywhere. Almost every house has a soak pit into which the wastewater is let. It is fully covered and the absence of the stench and mosquitoes is conspicuous. The houses ill-ventilated once, now admit light and air, thanks to the UBS authorities supplying 150 ventilators, free of cost. The households have fixed the ventilators at their own cost.

A beaming Mrs. Butramma proudly showed her buffalo for which she paid Rs. 500 and the Canara Bank gave a loan of Rs. 1,000. She had repaid the amount in six months. She was on the look out for another buffalo.

Community Hall in Ganeshnagar

The Community Halls in Telugugeri, Ganeshnagar and Sanjaynagar are also under construction. In Sanjaynagar, inhabited mostly by hamalies, the women themselves volunteered to work as construction labourers. Only the mason's services were hired. The women secured stones from nearby hills for the foundation. They approached the men folk who had carts and were transporting sand for others and said, "Why not lend your carts to us at night? We will go to the hills and bring the stones needed.'' They replied, "You gather the stones at one place. We will bring the carts ourselves and transport the stones to the site." Gauramma, the Convenor of the committee and the members were elated by this response.

The community hall at Ganeshnagar is a well-ventilated one with large windows. A pucca RCC roof has been laid. Mrs. Balakistamma, the Convenor, has been taking keen interest. She motivated her husband, a carpenter by profession, to volunteer his services free of cost. The committee is to supply the necessary wood and other materials like hinges, screws and aldrops. Coconut saplings have been planted and when I was in Ganeshnagar a pipeline was being laid.

A local political leader had originally offered land for construction of the community hall. But when other members of his joint family dissuaded him from doing so, the Neighbourhood Committee decided to purchase 200 sq. yds. of land for Rs. 9,000. The families in the area contributed the amount. This was in addition to the sum of Rs. 5,000 which had to be contributed to be eligible to get the Rs. 15,000 from the UBS funds.

Wrong Signals

In one town, because no public contribution was forthcoming from the residents, a suggestion was made that the sum of Rs. 15,000 from the UBS funds be returned to the UNICEF. But the officer higher-up was not for refunding the amount. He said donations from others could be secured to construct the community hall. It was done and the people have been led to believe that they can get things done without lifting a little finger.

Group Work

The Nehru Poormen's colony, the Kalyani Neighbourhood Committee has helped six of its members to get loans from the UBS Revolving Fund. The women purchase chillies, coriander, turmeric, pepper etc. and after drying them in the sun, have them ground in the flourmill. They pack the ground powder in 100 gm. packets. They mix the different ingredients in proper proportion to prepare sambar and rasam powders. Their preparations are in good demand. Some houses specifically demand the masalas prepared by the Kalyani NHC as the printed label inserted into each packet says. The Women's Hostel of the Sri Krishna Devaraya University also patronises them. When bulk quantities are required the products are sold loose.

Miss N.K. Aruna Jyothi, a Community Organiser, said the cooperative effort had been on since January last. What is to be admired is that though each lady is incharge of a separate item, they all sit together and pack them in packets. They also go together to market to sell the products and share the profits equally. Laxmi Bai, a tribal, prepares turmeric powder, Rabia gets the chillies ground, Sakkubai prepares the rasam powder, Rukmini Bai prepares the sambar powder and Jayamma is incharge of making leaf plates.

The Kalyani Neighbourhood Committee has been allotted a sewing machine. It has acquired two more, paying a rent of Rs. 50 per month for each machine. The Andhra Pradesh State Government's Scheme of supplying free shirts to rickshaw pullers has helped the women to stitch the shirts. Some women stitch as many as 20 shirts a day. For each shirt stitched, Rs. 1.50 is paid. The women thus make between Rs. 150 to Rs. 900 a month individually. They employ other women and pay them for stitching the buttonholes and the buttons. As the State Government's Social Welfare Department also seeks their help to stitch uniforms for the inmates of the various hostels, the Kalyani Neighbourhood Committee's members are assured of a steady income.

Public contribution to the construction of the community halls has been negligible. The Scheduled Castes Finance Corporation was asked to take up the construction of the halls. Only in Fazilbegpet the people contributed Rs. 2,000, so that a pucca RCC roof could be laid. In other places, asbestos sheets provide the roof.

Negative Attitude

In Fazilbegpet, some women have been trained to make masalas, mixing ground spices for cooking purposes. The women are not putting to use what they have learnt. Asked why the women should not come together and prepare masala on a cooperative basis and share the profits, as was being done in the Poormen's colony of Anantapur town, Convenor of the NHC, posed a counter question. She asked "who will go to the market and bring chillies?" Obviously, one of the women would have to do it. If that question were to be answered, it looked as if she might next ask "Who will grind the chillies and who will pack the masalas?" The UBS authorities can only provide the guidance, as also some loan and show the way. It is for the women to follow it. No one can hope to get benefits without working for it.

When suggested that the women could get loans from the banks also, it was pointed out that this avenue was closed to them.

She said many in the area had already taken loans but had not repaid them. Therefore, the banks evinced no interest in providing them more loans. The defaulters included some members of the Neighbourhood Committee! Hence, the recommendation of the Committee carried no weight.

Why were they not repaying the loans? An old lady replied "Indiramma said don't pay the loans, so we did not repay". Whoever was responsible for urging them not to pay, others in the locality are the sufferers as the banks have shut their doors to them.

The present NHC members have been there since the last 18 months. How and why all of them have been allowed to continue for a second term is not clear.

If some women were trained to make masalas and are not benefiting, the women of Golkonda Revu Road slum on the bank of the river Nagavali, are idle too after being trained to make coir ropes. Not one or two, but thirty women were given training for three full months.

Were all of them really interested to learn a new technique and put it to practice? I doubt very much.

Mrs. Mallamma, Mrs. Kamala and Miss Venkataratnam emphatically said that they were told by the concerned Community Organiser, Mrs. K. Sreelata, that they would be paid Rs. 4 per day during the training period. It was not done. They demanded that each of the thirty women who attended the training programme for 90 days be paid Rs. 360.

The women were told that a coir making machine, costing about Rs. 800 could be made available to them. But they were not interested in it. "We cannot work together," they said, "We want to work individually.'' A coir making machine would necessitate a group of women working on a cooperative basis. They did not want such an arrangement!

Community Hall by Wrong Way

In an old slum area in Srikakulam there is a community hall, near the main road. Women and children were watching a movie on TV, it being a Saturday. Mr. Paul, one of the residents, complained that the asbestos roof was leaking. He felt the contractor had not done his job properly. That happened because there was no community participation in the construction of the community hall. They could not supervise the work. The hall is the venue for the balwadi, sewing centre and female literacy classes. The beneficiaries, who were given loans, are now petty traders. There were no latrines in the area.

Mrs. Lingamma's Success in Kitchen Garden

Mrs. Lingamma showed her kitchen garden that she had laid out with a loan of Rs. 500. She had dug a well in a corner of her three-gunta land. Water was available at a depth of just seven feet. Her husband, Yankanna, is a mason but he gets work only occasionally. He used to waste his time sitting at the adda, hoping to get a call for work from someone or the other. He was also at home when I happened to visit the place. He was emphatic in declaring "Our troubles are now over". The kitchen garden yields Rs. 10 a day. Lingamma returned Rs. 5 every day to the bank. "I will be very shortly". The land was lying barren for decades. They grew beans, ladies fingers and green leafy vegetables. The chikkadikai (beans) plant, alone yielded 10 kgs, per week and I was able to sell it at Rs. 4 per kg." To supplement her income, Lingamma also has a buffalo, which helps her to get an additional Rs. 10 every day.

Lingamma's success has drawn more attention to the scheme than all the publicity by the authorities concerned. Her achievement is there for all to see. No wonder several others have approached Mr. Promod Kumar, Community Organiser, to secure loans for them. They have come to believe that the darkness that enveloped their lives is about to end. They see a ray of hope in the UBS. They have become aware of the benefits of the scheme.

Mrs. Mangthi

Mrs. Mangthi, a Resident Community volunteer, said they were saving two hours every day now, as they did not have to go in search of water. How did they utilise that time? She replied "By learning about cleanliness, health and hygiene and nutrition." Mangthi pointed out that their children did not "eat mud" any more. They had fitted ventilators to their houses and twelve families had the Barpalli type of latrines. "We have given up our traditional dress which was a hindrance to keep ourselves clean. We take a bath every day now."

At the Adult Education Centre, women were able to read newspapers after attending classes for a year. The Neighbourhood Committee was able to make the residents participate in cultural programmes organised during Independence and Republic Day celebrations.

The drains have been made pucca. Some months ago, it was difficult to walk along the lanes as the wastewater from the houses used to flow on to the lanes and make the area slushy. The residents have themselves levelled the area and dug a drain. A tractor was pressed into service to bring murram to construct the road. About a dozen women have learnt to ride bicycles. They do not wait for the bus, which is very crowded, to go to the town.

Handloom Weaving in Linewada

In Linewada, eight women have been given loans to help them carry on their handloom weaving. "We used to secure loans from the moneylenders at exorbitant rates and sell the dhotis that we weave at Rs. 22 per pair. Now, we are not only paying less interest, but are able to sell the dhotis at Rs. 26 a pair."

As the women were busy at their looms, their infants were sleeping in cradles closeby. The women were able to keep a watch over the children.

"We have been greatly benefited," declared women in the Perapalla basti neighbourhood. "We have had roads, drains, two public taps, one bore well, a balwadi and a sewing centre. Of course, we know there are greater goals to be achieved and we will endeavour to achieve them."

Mrs. Parvatamma with Pigeons

Mrs. Parvatamma of Srinivasanagar was able to have a flying start to her business of rearing pigeons. She has over 200 of them. She was a pigeon fancier, who bred pigeons for racing. The pigeons reared by her were the first to return home when released in Tirupati, Nandyal and Cuddapah. They took 2½ hours to fly back home from Tirupati, 1½ hours from Nandyal and 30 minutes from Cuddapah, covering the distance in lesser time than it took one in a motor car.

"Do the pigeons always come back?" I asked. Mrs. Parvathamma suggested "I take one to Hyderabad and release it there". I told her I was due to visit other places before going to Hyderabad. Since she insisted, I took a pigeon. I said I would take it to the Guest-House in Proddatur itself where I was staying and release it. I took one and tied a piece of paper around one of its legs. I had scribbled a small note in the paper. Half an hour after I released the pigeon, the chit was brought back to me, I had written. "This will not come back." However, the moment I released the pigeon I knew the note would come back, as immediately on being released, the pigeon flew straight in the direction of Srinivasanagar, though I had released it in the opposite direction.

Mrs. Shyamala is a Happy Young Woman

The boy, hardly five years old, tossed the 25 paise coin into the air and catching it in his right palm, even as it was falling down, put it on the ground with his right hand covering it completely. The boy opposite him, who must have been four years old, said "Chit," meaning head. The boy, who had tossed the coin, removed his hand and shouted, "It is pat". (Tails). He had won. The other boy had lost. The second boy passed on a 10 paise coin to the first one.

It was a gamble, pure and simple. But this type of gambling was very popular among the boys of the harijanwada, a slum area, in Tadipatri, a municipal town in Anantapur district. In the instance cited, the stake was just ten paise. In some others it was 25 paise. In yet other cases it ranged from 50 paise to 1 rupee, depending on the age of the participants. The boys sat in the shade of trees, or beside walls which threw a shadow. They could be seen all over, gambling and gambling. It continued from morning till late in the night. The game was interrupted when a policeman chanced to pass that way. Or, when the caller accused the tosser of indulging in unfair play. Then hell broke loose. Not only the two participants but their supporters also involved themselves in a free for all. Occasionally, a knife was whipped. There was blood. The sound of police whistles made all run helter skelter.

The boy who had no more money to lose, left the scene quietly, to look for some more coins. He tried to get them back by hook or crook. If found removing money, which parents had hidden away in the family hut, foul language was heard. The parents cursed the boy, even wished he were dead. But all that fell on deaf ears. At the end of the day everything was forgotten, with the men drowning themselves in liquor.

For the women folk, it was disgusting and unbearable. There was little that they could do. That is, until the Urban Basic Services Programme was introduced to them. The Ambedkar Neighbourhood Committee was formed. The women were asked "What is your most urgent need to be met; your most pressing problem to be solved? They did not ask for any amenities. They wanted to be rid of the obnoxious habits of their children. Some were just three years old when they started getting involved in the gambling game. "When children in other places are going to school, we are ashamed that our children should while away their time in such a useless game." A balwadi was started and the parents were urged to forcibly bring their children. It took sometime. But the formation of the Neighbourhood Committee is now a thing of the past in the Tadipatri Harijanwada. As many as 48 boys in the age group 3 to 6 attend the balwadi. Mrs. R. Shyamala, the balwadi teacher, is a happy young woman. She nodded her head as other women of the locality recounted the past and told me "This is the greatest benefit we have derived under the UBS programme."

The Government school is far away and we were afraid to send the children to that school, especially as they had to cross the highway connecting Tadipatri and Cuddapah. The traffic is very heavy, what with buses and lorries plying frequently. "Taking advantage of their parents' anxiety for their lives, the children never went to school but wasted their time in gambling. It was an unusual narration of the gains that the UBS had provided them. But it was a real gain and one had to hear the choking voices of the grateful women to realise how beholden they are to the UBS. Not only were they helped to eradicate an undesirable practice, but the children were also being helped to get a proper foundation for a better future. The women were happy and the children were more so.

Overcoming the Backlog

Ramalaxmi had never gone to school, "when I was a child, there was no anganwadi or balwadi. Neither was there a non-formal education centre. I could not go to school and had to attend to household chores. I am trying to make up and gain what I had missed in my childhood. I am grateful to the UBS for giving me the opportunity to realise what I had missed." She had attended the first batch of sewing centre and is now quite proficient. Now she wants to run a cooperative along with others.

Ms. M. Srilata, Community Health Volunteer

Miss M. Srilata who has had health care training, has treated over 30 cases of headache, fever, stomachache, vomiting, conjunctivitis and wounds, among the children and women. Carrying a First Aid Kit, supplied by UNICEF, she was seen putting eye-drops in the eyes of a boy having conjunctivitis. While the boy's mother was holding him, he himself was clutching a pet puppy, even as he was bawling out at the thought of someone putting something into his eyes.

Pride filled Alivelu Amma

Mrs. Alivelu Amma, who is 52 years old, has had training as a dai. "I do not have any record of the number of deliveries I have conducted during the last 25 years. The training I received last year has been useful in that I am able to sterilise the blade and other appliances that I use." "How much money was she making from attending the deliveries" Alivelu Amma was surprised. "Money"? She asked. "I attend deliveries so that I could accumulate some 'punyam' for the members of my family. I do not want anything more." Unlike some others in the profession, she was not working for the sake of financial gains. She was more than satisfied to render service to the women during the most trying periods of their lives.

Wonders in No Time by Gopalamma

The Convenor of the Neighbourhood Committee under the Urban Basic Services Programme, is Gopalamma who was elected just three months ago. Gopalamma has really brought wonders in the locality. She has had the community hall electrified within a week of her taking over.

The Municipality built the latrine much earlier but the municipal scavenger was not very regular in attendance. At any rate, he never turned up on Sundays and public holidays. But the calls of nature do not observe holidays and the community latrine became unusable whenever the scavenger did not turn up.

Last month, Gopalamma had a scavenger woman appointed on a salary of Rs. 250 per month, to be paid out of the UBS funds. The latrine and the surroundings are now very clean. Gopalamma said "We have converted the bucket-type, manual latrine into the flush-out type and have connected it to a septic tank." She was very happy to announce that all those using the latrines had been educated to flush out, before and after use. The community now claims "this latrine is ours — let us all keep it clean".

Television

The black and white TV set cost Rs. 3,000. While the UBS gave 75 per cent of the cost, the Neighbourhood Committee contributed the balance. The installation of the TV set has resulted in a bonus — it has attracted the women of the pig-rearing community in the locality. You may ask, "What is so wonderful about it? There are about a hundred families whose main occupation is to rear pigs. Like the animals they rear, the families are also known for their unclean habits. When some of their women wanted to see the TV programmes, the Committee said it had no objection but they would have to be clean. The habit of taking a bath was instilled in them. Now, about a dozen women turn up to watch the programmes after fulfilling the conditions. The need for cleanliness is slowly spreading in the community. A bath is seen no more as a luxury but a necessity.

Have they learnt anything by seeing the TV programmes or is it only the movies or the epics, Mahabharata and Ramayana, that are telecast that attracts them? A blushing woman in her 20's said, "I have learnt that giving birth to children frequently is not good either for the mother or her children.'' The women indeed are learning. Their knowledge is increasing. They are becoming aware of the needs of the day.

Street Light

The tubelight in the locality's lamppost had fused months ago and nobody bothered to replace it. Enquiries showed that the Municipality did not have the necessary fittings, which needed to be changed. The official offered to obtain 15 per cent of the money from the UBS provided the people raised the balance. The NHC then and there did it and within a couple of days, the street light was on.

Adult Education Centre

Twenty-nine adult women have been attending the adult education classes. One of them reported that Gopalamma herself went to the houses of the women and brought them to the community hall, keeping them in good humour. The adult education centre has been active since then.

Toddy Shop

The Neighbourhood Committee is not only active but vocal, too. It demanded that the toddy shop in the locality be removed. The authorities were forced to shift it. "But it has been shifted to just across the road and we are demanding that it be removed to a far away place", the women told me. They have become aware of the evils of drink but the men folk are somewhat adamant. They say they are earning and claim the right to spend the money the way they want. However, the women folk sounded confident — "we will succeed one day".

First Aid

Sarojamma is one of the five middle-aged women, who attended a training programme in First Aid. She remarked, "We used to be frightened whenever infants and children started purging. We prevented women from giving them food; especially liquid diet as we thought it would aggravate the loose motions. But after the training classes, we have changed our views. We are educating the women to give a pinch of salt and a spoonful of sugar mixed in water that was earlier boiled and then cooled." A delighted Sarojamma said, “We have saved four children ourselves and sent one to the hospital as it was a very acute case. That child also has survived.”

✪

4

Urban Basic Services in Orissa Towns

Can NHC Appoint its Own Teachers and Workers?

Balwadis are functioning in 16 of the 40 slums in the Keonjhargarh. The Notified area council had appointed all the balwadi teachers. When it is realised that it was only the Neighbourhood Committees that had the power to appoint the teachers, it promptly withdrew the appointment order. The NHCs reappointed most of the earlier teachers except three on the score that they were irregular in attendance. The three NHCs concerned — Sathighar, Nalaghat and Kashipur — have decided to appoint new teachers.

The former teachers are questioning the right of the NHCs to appoint teachers. They claim they are Municipal employees and so demanded pay scale prevailing in the Municipality. This is wrong. It is the NHC that plans, implements and manages its own affairs.

Alcoholism

Nearly 25 per cent of the slum population are casual workers of the Steel Plant in Rourkela. According to one official "if the average earnings of the slum dwellers is considered, their economic condition would not appear bad but alcoholism, to which more than 60 per cent of the male adults are addicted, is the real malady of slum life.

Mrs. Teja Nayak has undergone tubectomy though she has two daughters only. She said, "my husband is a drunkard. I did not want more children, as feeding them is a problem.''

Rice Business

Where there is a will there is a way. Whether individually or collectively, women have displayed grit and determination. Mrs. Rama Devi, a sixty-year-old woman, in Gopalbandhupalli slum, has battled against adversity to make a living. Her husband is too old to work. Their eldest son got married and promptly left home to set up a separate establishment elsewhere, forgetting his duty to his aged parents. Mrs. Rama Devi did not curse her fate. She did not take to begging. Spurred by the area's Community Organizer she applied for and got a loan from the Revolving Fund. She started doing business in rice and made a profit of Rs. 25 per day. That money came in handy "not only to keep our hearth burning but also to educate my second son." He had appeared for Degree examination and was awaiting the results. She is hoping that at least he would look after his parents. If he gets a job "hamaray bhi dhin bun jayenge."

UBS Bicycle

A building rented at Rs. 30 per month houses the balwadi in Harijanpara. A UBS bicycle has enabled many girls to learn riding the vehicle. This enables them to go to town that is quite some distance away.

Mela

The Additional District Magistrate, Mr. Kshetra Basi Kar is the District Coordinator for UBS programmes. He is taking keen interest and every month has a review meeting to monitor the progress. He was mainly responsible for organizing a Mela in Rourkela town. The beneficiaries from Rourkela and Sundergarh participated in the Mela. Besides having stalls displaying and selling the wares produced by the beneficiaries, there were sports for children and cultural programmes. The mela helped to bring to the notice of the people what the UBS is doing to the slum dwellers.

Negative Stake holders — Men

(a) If there is any lesson to be learnt from the implementation of the UBS Programme in Samalpur district of Orissa State, it is that it would be advantageous to involve the men folk also, to some extent. There is need to convince the men that when their women and children are benefited, they themselves would be benefited. The women and children are not living in isolation and if their condition improves, the entire family would benefit. Any advantage that the children and women derive will, naturally, reflect in the economic standards of the family. The entire family will share the benefits. All would be able to have better dresses, better health, better nutrition, better sanitation and better living standards.

(b) When I visited the community hall, a number of women trooped in. Soon there were some men too. As the women began to enumerate the advantages they had derived from the UBS programme, the men began to shout, "we do not want this community hall we don't need a balwadi. We don't want an Adult Education Centre here.'' It took quite sometime to calm them down.

(c) The women pointed out that when they began digging to lay the foundation for the community hall, some of the men laughed derisively and exclaimed the hall would never be completed. They swore, "we will shave off our moustaches if and when the hall is completed. But they have not kept their word."

(d) In Burla town some of the men expressed themselves against the new borewell that has come up in the area. They want their women to continue to trek a kilometer or two to fetch water. They feel that because the women folk had more time at their disposal they were "able to think of meetings and making great plans." The men were also opposing the installation of latrines. The pans were being supplied free alongwith three RCC rings. Yet the men did not want them.

Political Manipulations

Unfortunately, some politicians have been aiding and abetting the people. Quote — Some Municipal Councilors in Municipalities have told the people "You need not pay." The UBS will give

Rs. 15,000 for the community hall. Either the Municipality will pay the balance of Rs. 5,000 or it will get someone to donate the amount." Often, the contractor told him, "there is a piece of land in XXX colony, earmarked for a community hall. We can give you Rs. 15,000. You must complete the building. It may cost you more but we cannot pay from the Municipal funds. I will see that you are more than compensated when I give you some other official Municipal work."

Quote — Some community halls have come up, but without the people's active participation. They contributed neither one rupee nor lifted a single brick. It is the Contractors' men who did all the work. The very purpose of the UBS programme, of involving the community in the programmes is lost when the people are told they need not pay or participate in the construction. (Perhaps, all they are required to do is to vote for the politician concerned at the next elections.)

Such a convention is bad. There are instances where the Ward Councilor has wanted the community hall for holding (political) party meetings "as this building became a reality because of my efforts." The NHC had to yield and allow the use of the premises. Yesterday, the hall was wanted for a party meeting. It may be required this EVENING for a gala party and tomorrow NIGHT it might be required for some other purpose. Should such a thing be allowed? Political interference in the UBS functioning is to be seen in some places. I was given to understand that after the list of people in whose houses individual latrines were to be installed was finalised, approved by those concerned and notified to the persons themselves, the elected Chairman asked the Community Organiser concerned to change the list and provide latrines to the people of his choice. When the Community Organiser pointed out that the persons concerned have already been intimated and revising the list would mean facing their wrath, the Chairman threatened "I will see your end."

Special Class of Poor by itself

All those living in the notified areas are not among the poorest of the poor. There are factory workers, Class IV government employees, Municipal sweepers and scavengers who each get nearly Rs. 1,500 per month. They have a regular and sizable income compared to others. But they are not prepared to part with even a little of their income. The Government gave them pattas and regularised the ownership. The people do not want to have individual latrines or even drains. They want free education for their children, free clothing and free food. They want a creche but want the UBS to pay the ayah. They want milk and other food to be provided to the infants in the creche free. "When you are giving the children in the Vadiyala badis and Pindi Badis something to eat, why should you not provide the children in the creche free milk?" The anganwadis run under the Integrated Child Development Scheme give Ready-To-Eat food to the school students. It is these anganwadis that are referred to by the people as Vadiyalu (snacks) and Pindi (milk powder) schools. They want their children to be taken care of, so that they themselves could go out and earn but are not prepared to spare a naya paisa for their children to be looked after. There is need to bring about a change in the mental attitude of such people.

Mumtaz Begum (Idlis)

Among those who benefited by the Revolving Funds was Mrs. Mumtaz Begum. She had been preparing and selling idlis in the marketplace for the last three years but was not able to meet the demand. With a loan from the UBS she bought extra pots and vessels which helped her to prepare more idlis. She owns a pushcart in which she makes the snacks. Recently she opened a second centre, near a cinema hall. Her brother, a school drop out, helps her in running the business.

Mrs. Brunda Battinag : (Bangles)

Which woman does not like to wear bangles, symbols of auspiciousness among many communities? And who does not like coloured glass bangles? Mrs. Brunda Battinag, Secretary of the Dak Bungalow NHC, decided to avail the facility when the Community Organizer, Miss Aparna Padhee, said loans could be made available to some members. Till then she had not earned a paisa. With a loan of Rs. 200 she bought glass bangles and spread them in front of her house. She was able to make a profit of Rs. 20 a day. It enabled her to manage the household with greater ease. She was able to send her daughter to school and provide her better clothes and nutrition. A mother of five, she had undergone tubectomy. When people needed bangles urgently they even came to her house at odd hours. During the four-day Seetal Santi festival in June, she was able to secure a profit, which she normally earned in a month.

Why did she go in for selling bangles? She said that glass bangles often broke and people bought again. Since it was an item that people bought again and again, she decided to sell bangles. She did not regret her decision. She had begun in a small way and was now quite satisfied with the turnover.

Creche in Kuchinda

Small is beautiful. Kuchinda, is the smallest town in Sambalpur district with a population of about 9,400. There are seven notified slum areas and six NHCs; the total slum population is a little less than 4,000 with Scheduled Tribes accounting for 52 per cent. Though it is a D category town, with slum population less than 4,000, this NAC can boast of the best creche in the entire district. Twenty-eight infants are brought every morning to the creche and left in the care of ayah Mrs. Guruvari Rao. The youngest child is just six-month-old. She looks after it from 8.00 a.m. to 11.00 a.m. The mother takes away the child thereafter, she being busy for just three hours in the morning.

Ask any mother and she will tell you how difficult it is to take care of an infant. The mother of twins will express the trouble she has to undergo in attending to two infants. How much more difficult it must be for Mrs. Guruvari Rao to look after 28 children at a time! Few mothers leave some food for their children. For the others, the ayah mixes water and sugar and feeds them with it. Mrs. Rao explained that the tribal women were too poor to make any contribution.

Community Hall at Gayatrinagar

Kuchinda is an example of what can be done when the chairman, the Executive Officer and the Community Organizer put their heads and shoulders together. Branjrajnagar is an example of how stagnation would result if the Chairman does not recognize

TUBEWELLS UNDER URBAN BASIC SERVICES

the basic fact that community participation is a must in the UBS programmes. The work on community hall had come to a standstill because the Chairman of the NAC wants to complete them through contractors. The Executive Officer rightly opposed the move. The foundation for the hall was yet to be laid, though the pits were dug up a couple of months ago, a truck load of sand was unloaded at the site but since the work did not commence some unknown persons had taken it away. This was a loss to the community. Granite stones had arrived and the residents were finding it difficult to see that they were not carted away. In Gayatrinagar, the bricks had also arrived but they were safely stored in the residence of an RCV.

Borewell in Penthakota, Puri

"Water, water everywhere but not a drop to drink." That was what the fishermen who set out in their boats to catch fish in the Bay of Bengal experienced. The experience of their women folk who lived in Penthakota slum in Puri Town, on the shore of the sea, was no different. The vast expanse of the sea was before them, but they also did not have drinking water.

A businessman was quick to exploit the situation. He had three tubewells sunk. It was not very difficult to install the hand-operated pumps manually, the area being sandy. The men came and drove the pipes into the earth, hitting them with hammers. Water was struck at 20 feet. Every family was made to pay Rs. 10 per month to collect the tubewell water. There are 1648 households in the area, one of the biggest slums in Puri. Indeed, it is estimated that half the slum population of Puri lives in this area. The businessman spends only Rs. 1,000 for each of the borewells. He made a fortune within a short time.

The slum dwellers submitted themselves meekly to this exploitation. All of them being fishermen, who themselves are an exploited lot, there was little they could do. But the situation changed suddenly and the man invited the people to use his handpumps without asking for any payment. A sudden change of heart? A realization that he should serve the people? Nothing of the sort. The UBS authorities provided 13 tubewells in the area. When the slum dwellers were able to get water without having to pay for it, who would go to the borewells where they had to shell out money?

There are four NHCs in the area already. One more is to be formed shortly. The Fishermen's Association (Sangam) has erected four temporary thatched roof community halls for the UBS. While in several other UBS-served slums, not only in Puri district but in many other districts of Orissa and Andhra Pradesh, it was found that only the UBS was giving Rs. 15,000 for the building of the community hall and that the people's contribution was generally, next to nothing, in Penthakota, the UBS was not required to spend any money. The people themselves put up the structures. Only the motivation and guidance came from the UBS. The people said, "we will utilize your money when we are able to build permanent community halls." The present President of the local NHC, also handled the Adult Education classes. She said sixteen persons were given loans but some were not very regular in repayment.

Community Hall in Ramachandi

In Ramachandi area, Puri the community hall is nearing completion. The residents have not waited for the community hall to be completed to start a balwadi. The children gather under a big banyan tree. The NHC hopes to complete the building before the onset of the monsoons. Ramachandi B area was clubbed with Ramachandi A slum until five months ago. Not only has the new NHC moved fast in the construction of the community hall and the starting of a balwadi, it is progressing in other spheres also. The Secretary, Mrs. Primilata Patnaik herself led other women in the construction of the hall. Mrs. Swarna Prabha, Mrs. Promila Vidya and others helped in digging the foundation. The entire place being sandy and the lanes narrow, the vehicles that brought bricks, cement and other building materials were forced to unload them at quite a distance from the site. The women carried the materials from that place to the construction site — a commendable example of community participation.

5

Urban Basic Services for the Poor (UBSP)

Urban Basic Services for the Poor (UBSP) is yet another programme initiated by Government of India on a large scale with high budget. The project workers here are taken on contract and the designation is also changed as Assistant Project Officers, promising them an ambitious future. This programme has also created a mid level community structure *viz.* Community Development Society (CDS) in between NHC and Town Level Management Committee, giving it a lot of importance. This has got its own advantages and disadvantages.

The programme of Urban Basic Services in India was initiated during the 7th plan period. The National Commission on Urbanization (NCU) recommended for its universalisation covering all the urban areas and based on this the Government revised it as Urban Basic Services for the Poor (UBSP).

It was anticipated that UBSP would initially target 2000 households in towns with 1 lakh population, 4000 families in towns with 2 lakh population, 6000 families in towns with 3 lakh population and 8000 families in towns with 4 lakh population and 10,000 families in cities with 5 lakh and above population.

The organisational framework remained the same as in the programme of Urban Basic Services. The Community Development Society (CDS) is considered as a formal association of NHCs at ward/town level based on community goals and objectives and it is supposed to be a registered organisation with the representatives of all its NHCs as its members supported by COs and NGO representatives, Sectoral Departments, Elected Representatives of the area, and some leading citizens as its honorary members.

The project administration is also similar to that of UBS; but for the change of designation of CO as APO. At town level there is a UPA cell which coordinates, plans and implements all UPA programmes such as UBS, UBSP, NRY, EIUS, LCS and other special schemes.

At district level the State Government has constituted DUDA with a full time District Project Officer (PO) duly supported by other staff to work under the guidance and supervision of the District Collector.

At the State Level there will be the State Urban Poverty Alleviation cell registered as State Urban Development Authority (SUDA) in the office of the CDMA under his control. It will have Specialities in the areas of Education, Health, Nutrition, Marketing, Social survey etc. along with supporting staff.

At National Level, the National Level Monitoring Committee (NLMC) is to monitor the progress of all UPA programmes in different States.

The planning process, training, Programme monitoring and review are somewhat same as in UBS. But it also provides for the involvement of NGOs in the areas of community organisation, cost effective and innovative mechanisms, information education and communication, research and documentation, training and reaching the underserved groups.

In eighth plan the cost of UBSP is shared by Centre and State in the ratio of 60 : 40. It relies on suitable community structures and seeks to provide gainful employment to the urban unemployed and underemployed.

It consists of two special schemes :

1. Urban Self-employment
2. Urban Wage Employment

Here CDS is given much importance and shall be the focal point for purpose of identification of beneficiaries, preparation of applications, monitoring of recovery etc. It will also identify viable projects suitable for the particular area. It also encourages thrift and credit societies. Rs. 100 per member is allowed for activities connected with CDSs. This provides assistance to individual urban poor, groups of urban poor through Development of Urban

Women and children in Urban Areas (DWCUA) as in (DWCRA) and training of beneficiaries for acquiring vocational and entrepreneurial skills.

6

Urban Basic Services for the Poor (UBSP) — Revised Guidelines

The Urban Basic Services Programme in India was initiated during the seventh five year plan period for urban poverty alleviation. The programme was funded by the central and state governments and the UNICEF. Based on the experience of implementing the Urban Basic Services (UBS) programme during the seventh plan period, and the recommendations of the NCU, the government revised it as "Urban Basic Services for the Poor" (UBSP) Programme and integrated it with other urban poverty alleviation programmes, namely, Environmental Improvement of Urban Slums (EIUS), Nehru Rozgar Yojana (NRY) and Low Cost Sanitation (LCS). The revised UBSP programme is under implementation in about 280 towns as of July 1994 and it was expected to cover 500 cities/ towns during the Eighth Plan.

The State and Centre will share their cost in the ratio of 25 : 75 and this SJSRY is applicable to all Urban Towns and is implemented on a whole town approach.

1. Objectives

1.1 Effective achievement of social sector goals : To provide a platform to other sectoral programmes with a view to facilitating effective and rapid achievement of social sectoral goals including those incorporated in the National Plan of Action (NPA) for children in cities and towns by targeting the poorest through the community based participatory processes in harmony with the provision of the 74th Constitutional Amendment Act.

1.2 Community organization, mobilization and empowerment : To establish and support self-reliant community based women's groups and other organizations to actively participate in planning, implementation and monitoring of community development programmes.

1.3 Convergence through sustainable support systems : To enhance the convergence process through —

* facilitating adequate and effective coverage of the urban poor in all urban programmes through information dissemination and exchange;
* evolving innovative approaches to partnerships across departments, private sector, NGOs and other potential actors for maximizing the coverage of urban poor for socio-economic development and improving their quality of life.
* Establishing linkages between community and city level planning and management structures through a systematic devolution of resources and responsibilities to match with community needs, capacities and efforts at resource mobilization.

2. Organizational Framework and Responsibilities

The programme promotes community organization with special focus on women with supporting and facilitating mechanisms responsive to the groups' needs of development with a view to mobilize appropriate resources, and move towards self-reliant community-based organization which link them with city and sectoral processes. The community organizations include Neighbourhood Groups (NHGs), Neighbourhood Development Committee (NDCs) or Neighbourhood Committee (NHCs) and Community Development Societies (CDSs).

2.1 Neighbourhood Group (NHG) is an informal association of women living in a mohalla or basti. Geographic contiguity and homogeneity should be the basis to carve out the boundaries of the NHGs. At least one woman resident among them, who is willing to serve as a volunteer should be selected as a Resident Community Volunteer (RCV) through community consensus or election or any other democratic process. There should be a change or rotation, if need be, of such volunteers at periodical intervals.

2.2 Neighbourhood Development Committee (NDC/NHC) is a more formal association of women from the above neighbourhood groups located in close proximity and as far as feasible within the same electoral ward. The committee should consist of all the RCVs from the neighbourhood groups. There can also be a provision for honorary membership without a voting right for COs, representatives of other programmes in the community like ICDS supervisor, school teacher, ANM, etc. The NHC may form special need-based sub-groups *i.e.* Primary Education, Health, Nutrition, Sports, Culture, etc. as and when required.

2.3 Community Development Societies (CDS) are formal association of the above NHCs at the ward or town level based on common goals and objectives. The society may consist of elected/ selected representatives of NHCs/NDCs, with honorary membership which should include Community Organizers, representatives of NGOs, Sectoral Departments, leading citizens, elected representatives of the area and other resource persons. The CDS would be responsible to :

(i) represent needs of all the communities, especially women and children;

(ii) liaise and link-up with agencies and departments to promote action in the community towards fulfilment of their needs;

(iii) identify specific training needs and arrange for their organization;

(iv) prepare community plans and proposals, mobilizing resources from the community, city or other sectoral departments.

The Community Development Societies should be registered under the Societies Registration Act to provide access to grant-in-aid under various schemes and for a wider financial and credit base.

Community Development Society (CDS) cannot be treated just as an apex body to the Neighbourhood Committees (NHCs) and its functions should be more that of a regulatory and promotive nature such as :

- Collecting taxes from the petty businesses in slums where the local body is unable to do so;
- Efficient utilization of services in the CDS areas, and making suitable recommendations to improve their quality;
- Protecting and upkeeping community assets and common utilities in the CDS area;
- Watching the performance of staff working in CDS area and increasing their efficiency;
- Training at CDS level.

One area level Municipal Officer can be the nodal person to help the CDS in proper functioning. CDS may be in one or more wards for which there is a chairperson with all ward counselors, local staff, NHC Convenors, and two other co-opted persons as the members. Some matching grant has to be provided to each CDS to promote people's involvement and participation on a wider scale. With marginal support, CDS may be encouraged to take care of its own sanitation, social forestry, primary health care and other programmes of a local nature in collaboration with NHCs within it.

As regarding flow of funds, there are too many levels which seriously hamper the smooth functioning and efficiency of the programme. As in old UBS, funds may directly flow from Government to towns with certain pre-set indicators and criteria and it should be insisted that NHCs will operate these funds supplementing them with their own contribution to accomplish their mini plan targets. CDS will also have its own budget to cater to area needs of a general nature.

NRY, EIUS, and ICDS must be closely linked up with CDS and NHCs and people's participation must be laid as a pre-condition in implementing these programmes too. The success and utility rate in NRY training now is poor because of stipend element, which is the main attraction to lure people through recommendation. Genuine people are hardly getting this benefit.

The objective behind SUWE is only wage employment as interpreted by urban local bodies and the assets out of those grants are not necessarily created in slums and in pockets inhabited by poor. This situation has to be corrected by issuing suitable orders.

As the NHC gets stronger, and more viable, the municipality should encourage banks to lend money to individual NHCs to facilitate giving small loans to NHC members on group guarantee basis. Repayment of instalments can be ensured as the NHC is having its account in the same bank and this goes a long way in meeting the financial needs of urban poor and enable the poorest to avail small loans, which is very difficult through banks now because of cumbersome procedures even for petty loans. This can encourage thrift and credit also in a big way and at the same time enhance the income of the NHC in many ways.

At the Town Level

There should be a Urban Poverty Alleviation (UPA) Cell under the charge of a Project Officer (PO) of the Urban Local Body (ULB). It is a coordinating body of all UPA programmes. It is responsible to generate local municipal contributions, promote linkages and convergence with all the Sectoral Departments. The Cell will coordinate, plan and implement all the UPA programmes such as UBS, UBSP, NRY, EIUS, LCs schemes for night shelters for urban pavement dwellers and other special schemes for SC, ST, women, etc.

At the District Level

The State Government will constitute District Urban Development Agencies (DUDAs) with a full time I.A.S. Officer to work under Collector as District Project Director (DUDA) duly supported by other necessary staff. This will fix responsibility as well as ensure convergence of inter-sectoral inputs at the district and town levels. The functions of DUDA/District Project Officer (UBSP) should include mainly to :

(i) develop a policy for urban poverty alleviation at the district level;

(ii) promote and facilitate convergence with the sectoral departments at district/town levels;

(iii) promote information and experience exchange within the district;

(iv) monitor city convergence plans and implementation at district level.

State Level

At the State level a programme implementation cell known at State UPA cell in the office of the Director and Commissioner of Municipal Administration, should be constituted to coordinate with the State Development departments as well as District Collectors, District Project Officer (DUDA), Municipalities and associated training institutions. This cell will be responsible for the implementation of UBSP/UPA programme(s) including review and approval of Municipal and District Action Plans pertaining to urban poverty alleviation. The Cell would be under the Director (Municipal Administration) and will have specialities in the areas of education, health, nutrition, marketing technology, social survey etc. along with other supporting staff. In those States where State Urban Development Agency (SUDA) is functioning with appropriate staff as implementing agency it will serve as the State UPA Cell but with a Director/Commissioner of Municipal Administration as the Chief Executive of SUDA supported by a full time Additional/ Special Director.

National Level

At the National Level, Ministry of Urban Development is the Nodal Agency. The work is looked after by the UPA division, headed by the Director/Deputy Director (UPA) under the overall charge of Jt. Secretary. The National Level Monitoring Committee (NLMC) monitors the progress of implementation of the UBSP programmes. The functions of the UPA division will include :

(i) developing integrated and comprehensive UPA policy in the context of 74th CAA and other national goals;

(ii) approval of state UPA plans, monitor and assess the state performance;

(iii) facilitate the process of convergence through linkages with sectoral ministries/departments;

(iv) provide technical support and formulate a training strategy;

(v) provide channels of information exchange in stages;

(vi) mobilize resources from donor agencies.

3. Financial Pattern

Continuity and sustainability are the basic principles of the UBSP strategy. During the VIII Five Year Plan period, the UBSP costs were shared between the Central and State Governments on a 60 : 40 basis. As the funds from the Government of India are time bound, there is a need to create a resource base for the communities to support the community structures and to create support for the support systems discussed earlier. The allocation of financial resources to the projects help to move towards these objectives.

The Vision of UBSP is not merely serving a few slum pockets. It is to benefit all urban dwellers with the active participation of all residents of the city to provide a Healthy and Productive Environment for everyone especially children and women.

4. Summary

The UBSP is more than a scheme in and of itself. It aims to promote community-based organizations in poor and undeveloped clusters in the cities and towns. It aims at ensuring that these groups receive the entitled Government services from central, state and municipal programmes. It provides for "gap" filling financial support until such ongoing programmes fully cover the target areas. And lastly; it provides for resources, matched with community and family investments in promoting the community itself to take ongoing responsibility for its improvement aiming at making these families and neighbourhoods full partners in city development.

It is emphasized that the first line of action is convergence with the responsible department/agency at city or district level. In cases of this not being immediately possible, UBSP resources are available based on community needs and interests for financial support on the assumption that the responsible department will arrange for appropriate support in two years.

7

Urban Basic Services for the Poor (UBSP) — A synoptic note given to Government for information and guidance

Currently, the projects are concentrating on just providing physical amenities to the urban poor that too provided through contractors. If this is the only objective, there is no need to launch UBSP as a separate programme. Only 25 per cent of the UBSP budget is meant for creating physical assets as per guidelines.

1. There are vast human resources untapped yet, which can be groomed well by properly organizing, educating and motivating people and ultimately stimulate those to fully participate in accomplishing the desired felt needs. This gives them the feeling of ownership and self-achievement which goes a long way in the maintenance of the assets and their future sustenance.
2. Development does not mean just roads, drains or latrines alone. It also means preventive health care, education, environmental upkeep, nutrition for the needy, economic and social uplift of the most deserving through social mobilization and demand creation. All these have a bearing on the awareness levels and behavioural attitudes of the local masses, which have to be tactfully changed through frequent contacts and timely guidance. Effective communication on these aspects is important from government level.

3. Women's groups, which have a concern for their own development and that of children, must be systematically organised into neighbourhood groups, neighbourhood committees to be ultimately integrated into community development societies. They must be educated well on their present role and future initiatives and given adequate opportunities to deal with their own affairs, with the government offering suitable back up support.

4. The programme has to be low cost with in-built community contribution and participation to create the feeling that it is achieved by them and the assets created are for themselves. There is no role for a contractor in UBSP, as such approaches tend to keep the people away from the programme.

8

Prime Minister's Integrated Urban Poverty Eradication Programme (PMIUPEP)

It is yet another Programme which did not last long. But it gave a lot of emphasis to NGO involvement.

UPACOR was asked to play the coordinating and monitoring role at State level to assess the quantum and quality of work at town level by the local NGOs and recommend suitable assistance from the government. COs could not be recruited in any of the PMIUPEP towns and they have to be content with the social workers engaged by the local NGOs to organize and strengthen the NHCs. CDS has to play a key role in the programme planning and implementation but not much could be materialized.

9

Scope of NGO Involvement in Town Urban Poverty Alleviation Programmes (UPAP)

1. **Identification of poor :** A local NGO can precisely handle this task making necessary deletions and supplementations by local consultations and avoid diversion of NRY benefits to other economic groups. All the 3 components in NRY *viz.* SUME, SUWE and skills training and Shelter Upgradation Loans (SHASU) are exclusively meant to benefit urban poor. Guidelines were issued to identify the poor as an exclusive group on the basis of socio-economic survey and non-economic parameters survey for which reports are already available in respective municipalities. They must be got approved by the concerned NDC and then placed before TTF/UPAP committee at town level. This basic information is very crucial to cater the needs of this right set of poor.
2. **Thrift groups :** Banks are reluctant to give SUME loans because of repayment problems and NGOs can motivate NDCs/Communities to form thrift groups and establish an effective link between Banks and Poor.
3. **Group loans :** Quantum of loans and repayment terms are also unrealistic and with unduly long instalments. NGOs can make them more realistic in consultation with NDCs. Because of cumbersome procedures, banks are averse to advance small loans. NGO can identify small women's groups in each NDC as in DWCRA scheme and banks can give loans in lump sum amounts to

respective NDCs to cover the financial needs of these individual members in these groups. The loan will thus go to the NDC account which is jointly operated by NDC representative, Municipal Commissioner or his nominee and the NGO representative. Loan repayments in instalments can be paid from NDC account and the loanees can be made to pay their instalments with interest to NDC with the NDC & NGO acting as a pressure group. By this NDC can also make some marginal saving in agreement with the borrowers and NDC members (RCVs). Depending upon the need and the viability of the economic endeavours, more groups can be thought of in each NDC. Thus NGOs can promote thrift, social coherence and timely repayments to lending banks.

4. **Skills training :** Stipend has become more an attraction to undeserving youths. Training is also not need oriented. NGO can assess the real training needs and they can be got approved in the district level committee if necessary. Women should not lag behind in any skill. They must be made to feel that they are capable enough and are equal to men in every respect. They must be motivated to come forward for unconventional skills which have greater economic potential.

   NGOs can make women give up their reservations, shyness etc. and undergo training in new skills. NGOs can also identify good trainers, whether it be a training centre or a person for on-the-job training in consultation with municipality. They can also oversee the quality of training, assure continued interest of trainees and also ensure proper follow up after training. Stipend can also be utilized for a productive purpose after training. For all this the NGO is required to induct additional volunteers with some extra assistance from NRY funds which has to be prescribed in advance.

5. **EIUS and SUWE works :** 50 per cent of these funds may be set apart for developing community physical infrastructure in slums at the discretion of concerned NDCs and the remaining 50 per cent set apart for town

level infrastructure. We can insist on adequate community participation through shramadan which can be promoted by the concerned NGO. They can also motivate the NDCs in maintaining community assets for which Rs. 9,000 is provided to NDC for every Rs. 1,000 contributed by it as in PMIUPEP. Replacement of fused bulbs, taps etc., repairs to drains, community sanitation, tree painting etc., can be part of community maintenance activities. For social activities, a sum of Rs. 100 per capita is provided in PMIUPEP in 1st year and Rs. 75 in 2nd year. A portion of this provision can be utilized for physical infrastructure on a participatory basis which can again be motivated by NGO, and the rest for educational, social, health, recreational facilities etc. NGO can be an educator, motivator and facilitator in this whole process. But never a doer keeping the communities silent at the other end.

6. **Shelter upgradation :** It must be a beneficiary need oriented programme with his actual desires fully listed by NGO along with approximate costs. The beneficiary must be involved in making his own purchases under the guidance of NGO and he must feel he has done it with his own initiative and participation and it is a worthy investment. Rules and conditions for sanction of this loan may be relaxed if there is adequate assurance, about the genuinesess and repayment, from the NGO concerned.

7. **Community Kendras :** Rs. 1.00 lakh is only the upper limit in PMIUPEP. This must be the task of the concerned NDC with necessary motivational role played by the NGO to contribute at least 25 per cent in cash, kind or labour; entrusting it to a contractor will defeat our objective.

8. **Education :** Under the guidance of NGO, the NDC identifies the beneficiaries for creche, preschool, NFE and adult literacy programmes with special emphasis on girls and women. In line with the ongoing government assisted programmes, suitable remuneration may be fixed for the workers chosen from the locality or nearby area.

In the context of special reservations now made available for women, NGOs can also think of special coaching centres for girls and young women to qualify for Matric, Graduation etc. For these activities remuneration can be partly or fully met from NDC funds and accommodation insisted upon. For creches, the food that is normally given to the child at home has to be given in the centre by the mother in bottle or tin. These children can be given suitable supplementary nutrition on a participation basis. Play and sleeping equipment can be low cost and locally available.

9. **Low cost sanitation (L.C.S.) :** The procedure now in vogue is not giving fruitful results in terms of beneficiary satisfaction and involvement, proper usage or repayment of instalments. NGOs have tried different approaches with success and the municipalities should try out alternative methods to avoid this expenditure getting wasted. Trying small numbers of units with NDC involvement and NGO guidance supported by small advances to NDC may yield good results. Under sanitation package, NGOs in addition can motivate NDCs to construct soak-pits, washing platforms, toilets and baths, ventilators, smokeless chullahs and tree plantation, managing community sanitation etc. with suitable incentives from social activity and municipal funds. Community latrines are an eye sore in many municipalities and it cannot only be a criminal waste but also a dangerous source of infection and disease. They have to be repaired and renovated to the desired level using Municipal funds and involving the NDC. A token assistance may be given every month to NDC to engage a part time worker. NGO through user education can ensure its cleanliness and the NDC must feel the latrine is theirs.

10. **Health :**

1. *Under 5's Clinics* :

There are several interventions at community level which can promote child survival and help achieving summit goals by

2000 A.D. By utilizing the services of about 10-12 community health volunteers, under 5's clinics can be organized by NGOs offering the following services at fortnightly intervals at a convenient central point :

1. Growth monitoring for children upto 5 years to make mothers aware about proper growth of their children and the need for additional nutrition.
2. Oral rehydration therapy-demonstration and use of oral rehydration solution to mothers.
3. Education on breast feeding and weaning practices with demonstration on low cost locally available weaning foods to lactating mothers.
4. Offering immunization services to infants.
5. Distribution of Iron & Folic Acid tablets to children and pregnant women and low cost delivery kits for safe delivery at home if necessary.
6. Giving vitamin drops and deworming tablets to children upto 5 years, at regular intervals.
7. First aid for skin, eye, ear infections etc.
8. Family planning advice to mothers.
9. Education on low cost sanitary interventions at home like soak-pit, ventilators, smokeless chullahs, economic plants, washing platform, latrine, bath etc.

Each of the above counters can be handled by 1 or 2 Community Health Volunteers with a doctor and an ANM doing the technical part. Just like weekly shandis for vegetables etc., these clinics can be utilized by needy children and mothers at regular intervals after adequate motivation and education. This is a great community service which a NGO can promote.

2. *Training of adolescent girls and mothers* on preventive and promotive health care.
3. *Training of community health volunteers.*
4. *Eye camps, childhood disability camps etc.* in collaboration with Lions club and others.

COMMUNITY HEALTH VOLUNTEERS TRAINING

These can be planned by NGOs in consultation with NDCs and Municipal Commissioner and included in NDC miniplans.

11. **Recreational and cultural activities :** Competition in different skills and talents, games, sports exchange visits, study tours, cultural teams etc. can be planned at community and town levels to enthuse women, youth and children making provisions in NDC budget. There can be children's Mela, women's festival, youth jambori etc. once in a year at town level to boost the enthusiasm and participation of different groups.

12. **Strengthening and supporting NDCs and CDS** to chalkout plans and effectively perform their functions : CDS must make them the true implementers. NDCs must be registered as early as possible. To have effective checks, the cheques of NDCs may be signed by its representative and that of NGO and municipality. This requires effective guidance making things very transparent and NGOs must have a commitment to make NDCs confident, self-supportive and self-reliant in the long run. These attitudes are very essential on the part of NGOs, as they are only enablers and not doers.

13. **NGOs can also identify and develop special programmes for children and women in especially difficult circumstances** who include orphans, child delinquents, street children, child labour, disabled and destitute children, widows, deserted women etc. at town level soliciting UPAP funds.

14. **NGO is also a link and liaison** between poor and external agencies like revenue, health, social welfare, NEDCAP etc. to channel their services to the needy. They include pattas, ration cards, scholarships, pensions, civic amenities etc. to make the life of the poor meaningful and happy.

15. **Training and capacity building :** of grass-root level functionaries can be another function of NGO. To enhance general awareness amongst public, NGOs can promote

street plays, cultural teams, preparation of audio-visual publicity material for local as well as general use etc. Depending upon the local expertise and capability, NGO can take up one or more of above activities, work out human resources and material requirement at minimum levels and submit their budgets for assistance.

16. **In small towns it can take up a comprehensive area programme** as in PMIUPEP focussing on the following activities, which were adequately explained in above paras.

    1. Identification of the poor in the urban area and recommending the list to TTF after approval by NDC.
    2. Organise and strengthen NDCs and CDS in making their micro plans and implementing their programmes.
    3. Promote thrift groups.
    4. Recommend eligible beneficiaries for micro enterprise loans, shelter upgradation, skills training and LCS.
    5. Carry awareness programmes to motivate the poor for various developmental activities.
    6. Act as liaison between poor and outside developmental agencies including banks.
    7. Motivate poor on the need for education, mother and child health care, environmental sanitation, nutrition etc. which go a long way in achieving summit goals.
    8. Promote cultural and recreational activities through group melas and festivals.

10

Urban Poverty Alleviation Programmes (UPAP) — Involvement of NGOs and their Linkages with Local Bodies and above

Guidelines from UPACOR which acted as the Nodal Agency

Requests have come from many NGOs to assign them the task of working with the local poor in SEVERAL towns to promote social mobilization emphasizing activities related to Community Organization, motivation, self-employment, skills training, shelter upgradation, thrift etc.

Several Municipal Commissioners have finalized the list of NGOs and in the meetings convened by the Regional Directors of Municipal Administration, various matters related to preparation of budget, engagement of workers, performance of various tasks and submission of claims and their settlement were explained in detail to all the NGOs who participated in these meetings.

The following guidelines are emphasized to ensure smooth procedures for the guidance of Non-governmental Organizations and Municipal Commissioners In-charge of UPA programme :

1. Selection of NGOs and entrusting specific areas to each NGO, is the responsibility of the Municipal Commissioner in consultation with the chairperson.
2. Urban poor are not limited to slums and so an area has to be allotted to NGOs on a ward-wise basis.
3. Selection once made and communicated to UPACOR

cannot be changed and can be revoked only after a year unless something is absolutely faulty.

4. NGO budget is fixed at Re. 0.50 paise per capita of town population and expenditure over and above that, has to be borne by the NGO concerned.
5. The NGO has to submit a brief report of work done to Municipal Commissioners once a month with copy marked to UPACOR.
6. The first claim for the quarter has to incorporate the details of work done during the quarter, workers engaged with details of remuneration, qualification, age, date of commencement etc.
7. Expenditure incurred in a quarter should not exceed one-fourth of the annual budget already approved by Municipal Commissioner.
8. Each quarterly report from NGO has to go to UPACOR with a copy marked to Municipal Commissioner for his comments and recommendation for payment.
9. Reimbursement is done by commissioner or Director of Municipal Administration to the NGO on recommendation by UPACOR.
10. If there are 2 NGOs selected in a town and if one NGO amongst them is unregistered, the total claim is to be preferred by the other NGO, which is registered.
11. The Municipal Commissioner must convene fortnightly meetings for his UPAP staff and that of NGOs to ensure that the programme is going on right path and any procedural or implementation problems are sorted out.
12. The precise list of poor in all towns has to be approved by the concerned Neighbourhood Committee as well as town level task force committee. Beneficiaries for different loans have to be drawn from this list alone.
13. The NGO has to systematically form and strengthen the NHCs to efficiently perform their responsibilities.

11

The Swarna Jayanti Shaheri Rozgar Yojana (SJSRY)

The Swarna Jayanti Shahari Rozgar Yojana (SJSRY) shall seek to provide gainful employment to the urban unemployed or underemployed poor through encouraging the setting up of self-employment ventures or provision of wage employment. This programme will rely on creation of suitable community structures on the UBSP pattern and delivery of inputs under this programme shall be through the medium of urban local bodies and Neighbourhood community structures.

The Swarna Jayanti Shahari Rozgar Yojana was funded on a 75 : 25 basis between the Centre and the States.

The Swarna Jayanti Shahari Rozgar Yojana shall consist of two special schemes, namely :

(i) The Urban Self-Employment Programme (USEP)

(ii) The Urban Wage Employment Programme (UWEP).

Components of USEP

(i) Self-employment through setting up Micro-enterprises

(ii) Development of Women and Children in Urban Areas (DWCUA).

This scheme is distinguished by the special incentive extended to urban poor women who decide to set up self-employment ventures in a group as opposed to individual effort. Groups of urban poor women shall take up an economic activity suited to their skill, training, aptitude, and local conditions. Besides generation of income, this group strategy shall strive to empower the urban poor women by making them independent as also providing a facilitating atmosphere for self-employment.

To be eligible for subsidy under this scheme, the DWCUA group should consist of at least 10 urban poor woman. Before starting Income generating activity the group members must get to know each other well, understand the group strategy, and also recognize the strength and the potential of each member of the group. The group shall select an organizer from amongst the members. The group will also select its own activity. Care should be exercised in the selection of activity because the future of the group will rest wholly on an appropriate selection. As far as possible activities should be selected out of an identified shelf of projects for that area maintained by the Town Urban Poverty Eradication Cell. In addition, every effort will be made to encourage the group to set itself up as a thrift and credit society.

Financial Pattern

The DWCUA group society shall be entitled to a subsidy of Rs. 1,25,000 or 50 per cent of the cost of project whichever is less.

Where the DWCUA group sets itself up as a Thrift and Credit Society, in addition to its other entrepreneurial activity, the group/ Thrift and Credit society shall also be entitled to a lump sum grant of Rs. 25,000 as revolving fund at the rate of Rs. 1,000 maximum per member. This revolving fund shall be available to a simple Thrift and Credit Society also even if the society is not engaged in any project activity under DWCUA. This revolving fund is meant for the use of group/society for purposes like :

(i) Purchases of raw materials and marketing;

(ii) Infrastructure support for income generation and other group activities;

(iii) One time expense on child care activity. Recurring expenses like salary, for stall rent etc. will not be payable;

(iv) Expenses not exceeding Rs. 500 to meet travel costs of group members for visit to banks etc.

(v) Where an individual member of a Thrift and Credit

Society saves at least Rs. 500 in a fixed deposit for 12 months with the society, she will be entitled to a subsidy of Rs. 30 to be paid on her behalf towards a health/life/accident/any other insurance scheme for herself. Moreover, in cases where the member saves at least Rs. 750 in a fixed deposit for 12 months, she will be entitled to a subsidy of Rs. 60 at the rate of Rs. 30 for the member herself and another Rs. 30 for her husband towards health/life/accident/any other insurance or Rs. 30 for any minor girl child in her family for health/accident insurance. This expense may also be debited to the revolving fund; and

(vi) any other expense allowed by the State as being necessary in the group or society's interest.

A DWCUA group/Thrift and Credit society shall be entitled for payment of revolving fund not earlier than one year after its formation. In other words, only such a body in existence and functioning for at least one year shall be eligible for payment of the revolving fund. The decision whether a group has been in existence and functioning for more than one year shall be taken on the basis of examination of the record of the group in terms of the number of meetings held, the collections made from members towards group savings, the regularity of collection, the role of the group in capacity building or training of its members etc.

The Urban Wage Employment Programme (UWEP)

This programme shall seek to provide wage employment to beneficiaries living below the poverty line within the jurisdiction of urban local bodies by utilizing their labour for construction of socially and economically useful public assets.

This programme shall apply to urban local bodies, the population of which was less than 5 lakhs as per the 1994 census.

The material labour ratio for works under this programme shall be maintained at 60 : 40. The prevailing minimum wage rate, as notified from time to time for each area, shall be paid to beneficiaries under this programme.

Programme Implementation : is nearly similar to that in UBSP at all levels. But CDSs are given more importance.

Non-economic parameters to be considered for eligibility of a household for drawing benefits under SJSRY

PARAMETER		WEIGHTAGE SCORE FOR EACH ATTRIBUTE					
		100 (A)	80 (B)	60 (C)	40 (D)	20 (E)	0 (F)
1		2	3	4	5	6	7
(A)	LIVING CONDITION :						
(i)	ROOF	THATCH	TARPAULIN	ASBESTOS	WOODEN	TILES	CEMENT
(ii)	FLOOR	EARTHEN	BAJRI	BRICKS	CEMENT	CHIPS	STONE/ MARBLE
(iii)	WATER	NO WATER SUPPLY FOR 500 YARDS	COMMUNITY HAND PUMP	COMMUNITY TUBEWELL	PRIVATE HAND PUMP	PRIVATE TUBEWELL	PRIVATE PIPED WATER SUPPLY
(iv)	SANITATION	OPEN DEFE-CATION	COMMUNITY DRY LATERINE	COMMUNITY POUR FLUSH LATERINE	PRIVATE DRY LATERINE	PRIVATE POUR FLUSH	PRIVATE FLUSH LATERINE WITH SEWER CONNE-CTIONS

(B)	EDUCATIONAL LEVEL	ILLITERATE	PRIMARY PASS	MIDDLE PASS	MATRIC PASS	10+2 PASS	GRADUATE PASS
(C)	TYPE OF EMPLOYMENT	UNSKILLED CASUAL/LABOURER/ UNEMPLOYED	SEMI SKILLED	SELF-EMPLOYED STREET/ PUSH CART	OWN WORK PLACE	OWN WORK PLACE & SELLING PLACE	ORGANISED SECTOR WITH SOCIAL SECURITY
(D)	STATUS OF CHILDREN IN A HOUSE	WORKING CHILDREN & NOT ATTENDING ANY SCHOOL NFE/LITERACY CLASSES	WORKING CHILDREN BUT ATTENDING SCHOOL NFE/LITERACY CLASSES SOMETIMES	WORKING CHILDREN BUT ATTENDING SCHOOL NFE/LITERACY CLASSES REGULARLY	CHILDREN NOT WORKING AS WELL AS NOT ATTENDING CLASSES	CHILDREN NOT WORKING ATTENDING SCHOOL NFE/LITERACY CLASSES SOMETIMES	CHILDREN NOT WORKING ATTENDING SCHOOL NFE/LITERACY CLASSES REGULARLY

Note : This is a suggestive one. However, the Town UPE cell, in consultation, with CBOs concerned, can slightly modify the parameters based on local conditions/factors to identify the poorest of the poor in the town.

Procedure for Identifying an Urban Poor Household for Economic Benefits

As indicated, top priority should be given to those who are below the poverty line. But the old procedures of simply going by income certificates are not benefiting the real poor. So certain non-economic may also be considered for identifying a genuine beneficiary among urban poor for income generating special loan schemes under this programme. Seven non-economic parameters have been identified for this purpose. These include : (i) Roof, (ii) Floor, (iii) Water, (iv) Sanitation, (v) Educational level, (vi) Type of Employment, and (vii) Status of Children in a house.

12

Community Based Structures to be Set up Under SJSRY

The community based organizations include Neighbourhood Groups (NHGS); Neighbourhood Committees (NHCs) and Community Development Society (CDS).

1. Neighbourhood Group

This is an informal association of women living in a mohalla or basti or neighbourhood. Group of manageable size (preferably to 10 to 40 urban poor or slum families), geographic contiguity and homogeneity should be the basis to carve out the boundaries of the NHGs. One woman resident among them who is willing to serve as a volunteer should be selected as a Resident Community Volunteer (RCV) through community consensus or election or any other democratic process. There should be a change or rotation (if need be) of such volunteers at periodical intervals. The responsibilities of the RCVs include :

(i) to serve as a channel of information and communication among the families in the cluster;

(ii) to represent the views of the groups in the neighbourhood committees and community development societies and other forums;

(iii) to support planning, implementation and monitoring of activities at the neighbourhood level; and

(iv) to foster and encourage participation in community improvement;

(v) to motivate the community for being members of thrift

and credit society; and to contribute to community development fund.

2. Neighbour Committees (NHCs)

A neighbourhood committee (NHC) is a more formal association of women from the above neighbourhood groups located in close proximity and as far as feasible within the same electoral ward. The Committee should consist of all the RCVs from the neighbourhood groups as executive members (with voting right) of NHC as well as one female member (without voting right) from each family which falls under the jurisdiction of NHC concerned. There can also be provision for honorary membership without a voting right for community organizers (COs), representatives from school teachers, ANMs etc. The convener/ President of the NHC will be convener and will ensure that the meetings are convened on regular basis. The NHC would be responsible :

(i) to identify local problems and priorities;

(ii) to provide suggestions for groups involvement in meeting community needs and goals (mini-plans);

(iii) to support local action with partnership of responsible agencies including community contracts;

(iv) to provide feedback to agencies on programme effectiveness and out-reach especially for children and women;

(v) to develop community capacity through training in association with COs, NGOs and other sectoral departments;

(vi) to develop community based thrift and credit systems as well as neighbourhood development fund;

(vii) to facilitate the recovery of loans from the beneficiaries in time and

(viii) to assist/carry out community surveys in accordance with the guidelines.

The NHC may be registered under the Societies Registration Act, or other appropriate Acts if so desired. If registered, these NHCs may also apply for grants-in-aid under various schemes.

3. Community Development Society (CDS)

The CDS is a formal association of all the neighbourhood development committees at the town level based on common goals and objectives. The CDS may consist of elected/selected representatives of NHCs as executive members (with voting right) as well as one female member from each family (without voting right) which falls under the jurisdiction of CDS; and other members with honorary membership (with no voting right) which may include community organizers, representatives of NGOs, sectoral departments, leading citizens, elected representatives of the area and other resource persons. The Community Development Society (CDS) should be registered under the Societies Registration Act or other appropriate Acts to provide access to grant-in-aid under various schemes and for a wider financial and credit base. The CDS would be responsible :

(i) To represent needs of all the communities, especially women and children;

(ii) Liaise and link-up with Agencies and Departments to promote action in the community towards fulfilment of their needs;

(iii) To identify specific training's and arrange for their organization;

(iv) To facilitate community surveys to be carried out to identify the genuine beneficiaries for economic and shelter benefits.

(v) To prepare community plans and proposals, mobilizing resources from the community, town or other sectoral departments.

(vi) To extend help to banks in coordination with UPE Cell, for ensuring repayment of loans by the beneficiaries in time.

(vii) To create small community assets in low income areas in consultation with town UPE cell and Urban Local Body (ULB).

13

Community Contract System

Advantages

Generates employment for skilled, semi-skilled and under-skilled people in the community.

Ensures that amenities/services are needs-based

Ensures optimum utilization of time, money and labour

Ensures higher/better quality of services/amenities

Ensures proper maintenance and hence sustainability

Builds confidence of community and promotes self-reliance

Reduces the pressure on civic authorities

How/Process

NHC to identify the required amenity/service

Prepares proposal outlining the cost and processes with the help of CO/Municipal Engineer.

Submit proposal to town UPE cell

Once approval is given and first instalment of advance is released.

Establish committee for execution and monitoring of the contract.

Maintain and submit proper reports and accounts

Use profits for community activity

Potential Areas for Community Contract

Construction and maintenance of roads, pavements, drains, garbage pits, toilets, sewerage, hand pumps/piped water, community centres, NHC office, schools, health posts, worksheds, kiosks/ shops, low cost houses, smokeless chullahs etc.

Development of open spaces as parks, collectives for growing of vegetables, mushrooms, flowers etc.

Ponds for fish breeding.

Running and managing sanitation maintenance system, fair price shops, balwadis etc.

14

Prajala Vaddaku Palana (PVP) and Shramadan : A case study and a note on workable implementation in urban areas

PVP aims at improving government functioning :

- Improving the performance of Government Institutions and Municipalities.
- Quick redressal of public grievances
- Better quality of works at the Community/Town level
- Accountability of Government Institutions and Agencies
- Increased awareness of development programmes
- Effective functioning of Public Institutions like Schools, Hospitals and other Institutions.
- Transparency in Government Functioning :
    - Decisions regarding development schemes
    - Criteria and methods of Identification of beneficiaries
- Fixing Schedules/Targets for different Functionaries

PVP is a :

- New Development Approach
- Movement towards Sustainable Development
- People's Programme : Not an Official Programme
- Bottom up Planning : Not Top Down Planning

Objectives of PVP

- Taking Administration to people
- Visiting the communities regularly
- Meeting the felt needs of the people
- Grievance redressal and problem solving of community and individuals.
- Identify the problems and gaps in the delivery of services.
- Improving the functioning of local administration
- Community mobilization
- Micro Planning

As matters stand now, the governmental agencies want communities to participate in the programmes planned and implemented by them. Due to various reasons, this is not working and so the future strategy of the government should be to enable the communities to plan, implement and manage them, channeling their share of assistance to committees chosen by different communities. For the creation of any useful asset in the community, governmental agencies are willing to give 50 per cent assistance, which can be routed through one nodal agency, with the revenue department acting as a watchdog for utilisation and additional releases. Now we assume the municipality has got sufficient money to support PVP and shramadan in its limits.

Depending upon the social cohesiveness, the municipality can identify different pockets inhabited by the poor and instigate them to form a small committee to identify and solve their problems. Then how it raises its own resources is left to the option of the committee.

For an effective approach, let us take one particular committee as a case study :

An NGO has identified a homogenous Community, with over 100 families, having identical problems related to water, road, lights pattas, ration cards etc. At this stage they do not want to consider other problems like education, health, women's issues etc. as a priority, which the NGO very much respected. They were all made to sit together to form a committee. The assembly felt the collections and money dealings will be safer in the hands of women and so they chose office bearers from amongst women and also formed a men's wing committee, in addition, to support the women's group. In all there are 7 men and 7 women in the committee.

Then they discussed about their immediate problems and needs which are listed below. Drinking water is an acute problem. With the help of local MLA/MP, they are promised one water tanker every day. But the path way is very bad and the contractor is trying to avoid the trips.

(a) So they wanted to set right the road of over 1 km length spending about Rs. 3,000.

(b) They wanted to construct a sump with taps to avoid quarrels and wastage of water costing Rs. 3,000.

(c) They wanted to restore a tubewell by fixing drawing apparatus costing Rs. 2,000.

(d) The tube lights on the road side were burnt out six months ago and they wanted to replace all of them without waiting for municipal assistance.

Then the discussions went round funds mobilization. NGO said until such time the government gives a helping hand, it will keep Rs. 15,000 in the bank account of the committee to be operative by NGO representative and President/Secretary of the committee. But its utilization is subject to the condition that the committee puts in at least 50 per cent as their share either in cash or kind in advance. The gathering felt, it is difficult to collect contribution for each item separately and instead each family would pay Rs. 10 once every month regularly to the committee account as their share. In addition they would each pay Rs. 25 to make up their contribution for the needs on hand.

As promised, the NGO has put Rs. 15,000 and the whole process started working.

For credibility purpose the committee has purchased some tube lights and brought light to the community on the very next day. Now the committee is busy collecting their share and putting it in the bank kitty to accomplish their need.

The stimulating factors in this whole process are the NGO, the seed money deposit in the committee's account, the organisation as initial imprest (CBO) and its contribution.

Now the questions are :

1. Can the NGO organise the CBO and motivate them for self-help?
2. Can the governmental agency (municipality) repose confidence in NGO and CBO and release about Rs.10000 as initial imprest to the account of each of such committees?
3. Can the NGO motivate CBO members to fulfil their part?
4. Can the NGO slowly make the CBO focus their attention to invisible needs related to health, education, etc. in the long run aiming at summit goals and enable it to be self-reliant in every respect standing on its own legs?

I believe if we keep working assiduously and sincerely, our goals towards a better society will surely be achieved.

A LITTLE ABOUT THE AUTHOR'S PAST

(FOR THE INFORMATION OF YOUNGSTERS)

The author is from an agricultural family in a zamindari village in East Godavari District of Andhra Pradesh. His father was a village Munsiff, who had four younger brothers. They all with over 40 members lived in a joint family till he reached Middle School age. He still remembers his paternal grandmother sitting on a 3-legged stool and giving commands to her daughters-in-law regarding the daily chores. Her five sons shared work amicably amongst themselves under their elder brother's guidance. As village Munsiff, his father wielded much respect, both from villagers as well as the then British Government, which gave him a 'ponnukarra' (hand stick with silver handle) as a momento.

His father died when he was hardly ten years in age. The elderly support and guidance of his brother, Sri G. Satyanarayana Murty and the hard home work and affection bestowed by his beloved mother, late G. Seshamma and his sister-in-law, Smt. G. Krishnaveni enabled him to rise to this level with his continued education and effort.

The author's education upto 8th class was in the local Middle School, which hardly costed him Rs. 30 for 3 years. The rupee value was very high in the years — '30s and '40s when one bag of paddy used to cost just over Rs. 3 and a tola of gold (11 grams) around Rs. 80. Then came the High School education in a nearby town across river Godavari. A messenger used to get food from home twice a day and with just over Rs. 120 he was able to complete High School education.

In Colleges, the rules and procedures used to be very simple and one could get into any group without much difficulty. With hardly Rs. 500, he could get through the Intermediate course at

Kakinada. He then joined and successfully completed the four year Bachelor's degree in Veterinary Science (B.V.Sc.). The stipend of Rs. 30 p.m., during this period, enabled him to meet major part of his hostel expenditure.

After getting the degree, he was posted to a remote place in Kurnool district in 1952. He was the first in the family to enter into government service and he enjoyed his work there with a monthly salary of Rs. 173 and an annual increment of Rs. 5 then.

A time has come (1956) when the best in the Animal Husbandry Department were selected for National Extension Service (NES) blocks and he was one amongst them to be posted to Guntur district as Extension Officer. He was in this interesting job for 3 years. Thereafter he worked as Block Development Officer, which kept him busy till 1967. In between, his younger brother, Dr. G. Ramananda Rao, a post-doctoral fellow in United States explored the scope of his getting into MS and with his support, the author got his M.Ex. (Masters in Extension) from Washington State University in 1965. Though he got a job offer then, he preferred to get back to India and continue with his old profession.

The author was selected as Project Officer in Urban Community Development (UCD) in Municipal Corporation, Hyderabad in 1967 and his team of staff struggled hard for survival and recognition in that organisation, which was a big ocean with about 9000 employees. They slowly gained popularity and proved worthy to the extent of their big bosses realising the usefulness of the UCD programme and its need to solve the innate problems of urban poor. The rest is in this volume.

The success of UCD was because of two factors. The most important was the element of community participation and the strong conviction that every one can contribute and work for the betterment of his family and the community. Next is the team work. Some staff members were bold and daring while others were for cautious moves. There was respect and confidence in the leadership. The author specially owes his thanks to the continued support, timely and friendly advice of his colleague, Sri D.G. Rama Rau, who was with him in all his joys, sorrows and ambitious plans. Sri B. Yadagiri Reddi was a deep thinker and a good writer. Sri T. Papaiah used to be dashing in tune with his physique. Mr. Mahmood Ali had a legal vision. Amongst the lady Community Organisers, Mrs. T. Gayatri used to feel that nothing is impossible. Mrs. Subbayamma was sincere and committed. Mrs. Venkateswari followed the footsteps of her husband, Sri Rama Rau. The fourth one, Ms. Sarojini was there for a short time. The achievements they cherished were due to the joint effort of the entire team and the author owes his thanks to one and all of them.

UCD has grown to the extent of international acclaim in 1970's and the author got his voluntary retirement in 1980. He leaves it to the present generation to judge how the programme is today.